Conversational
ARABIC
in 7 Days

*Master Language Survival Skills
in Just One Week!*

Samy Abu-Taleb

McGraw·Hill

New York   Chicago   San Francisco   Lisbon   London   Madrid   Mexico City
Milan   New Delhi   San Juan   Seoul   Singapore   Sydney   Toronto

Originally published by Hodder & Stoughton Publishers.

1 2 3 4 5 6 7 8 9 0   WKT/WKT   2 1 0 9 8 7 6 5 4 3

ISBN 0-07-143266-3 (package)
      0-07-143265-5 (book)

Acknowledgments
The authors and publishers are grateful to J. Allan Cash Ltd. for supplying photographs.

McGraw-Hill books are available at special quantity discounts to use as premiums and sales promotions, or for use in corporate training programs. For more information, please write to the Director of Special Sales, Professional Publishing, McGraw-Hill, Two Penn Plaza, New York, NY 10121-2298. Or contact your local bookstore.

This book is printed on acid-free paper.

CONTENTS

INTRODUCTION

Arabic in a Week is a short course which will equip you to deal with
everyday situations when you visit any of the Arab countries: introducing
yourself, asking for directions, booking accommodation, changing money,
shopping, eating out, using the phone, using public transport and so on.

The course is divided into 7 units, each corresponding to a day of the
week. Different topics are introduced in each unit to illustrate basic
Arabic which can be used by tourists or business people during a short
stay in an Arabic speaking country. Each unit includes short introductions
to the topics covered, dialogues in everyday situations, lists of key words
and phrases with their English equivalent, essential grammatical
explanations, and exercises for practising spoken Arabic.

A key to exercises is given at the back of this book. English–Arabic
vocabulary is listed under topic headings pp. 79–85 followed by an
Arabic–English Vocabulary starting on p. 86.

What kind of Arabic?

There are two main varieties of Arabic: literary and colloquial. Literary
Arabic is more formal. In its written form, it is used in official documents,
newspapers, books, and formal letters. In its spoken form, it is used in
public speeches, religious sermons, radio and television news bulletins
and documentary programmes. Literary Arabic is standard and is used
and understood by educated people in all the Arab countries. A table of
the Arab countries is given on p. 91.

Colloquial Arabic is the spoken variety used for everyday purposes: at
home, in the shops, offices, hotels, restaurants and places of
entertainment. Due to the vast area of the Arab world, colloquial Arabic
varies from country to country. Nevertheless, the dialect used in Cairo (the
capital of Egypt) is recognised and understood almost everywhere in the
Arab world. It is known as Cairene or Egyptian Arabic. Almost everyone
in the Arab world is exposed to Egyptian Arabic as a result of listening to
Egyptian radio programmes, importing Egyptian television programmes,
videos and films and buying cassettes and records of Egyptian popular
songs. In addition, millions of Egyptians travel to other Arab countries and
millions of Arabs from other countries travel to Egypt for business,
education and holidays.

The Arabic taught in this book is Egyptian Arabic. Some words and
phrases which are used in non-Egyptian Arabic are also included
wherever appropriate.

Pronunciation

Most of the sounds of Arabic are similar to the sounds of English. Only six
or seven might be unfamiliar to English speakers. Arabic has its own
alphabet of 29 letters, and is usually written from right to left in its own
script (see p. 92).

INTRODUCTION

In this book, however, Arabic sounds are represented by English letters, and written from left to right. Some English capital letters are used to represent certain Arabic sounds different from those represented by the corresponding small letters.

Some key words which visitors to Arab countries might need to recognise on signs or notice-boards are also written in Arabic and are introduced in the relevant chapters of the book.

The sounds of Arabic are divided into vowels and consonants. **Vowels** are either short or long.

Short vowels

a   as in about, postman, e.g. samak (fish)
i   as in bit, his, e.g. bint (girl)
u   as in put, foot, e.g. ruzz (rice)

Long vowels

aa   as in hand, e.g. salaam (peace)
ee   as in feed, e.g. sheek (cheque)
ou   as in dome, e.g. youm (day)
oo   as in room, e.g. lamoon (lemon)
ei   as in name, e.g. beit (house)

Note: **a** and **aa** are both influenced by certain consonants near them. The word baTT, for example, is pronounced like the English but, because of the **T** sound. The aa in the word DaabiT is pronounced like the a in calm, because of the **D** sound.

Consonants

The following Arabic consonants are similar to English ones.

b	book	**g**	game	**l**	look
d	day	**h**	home	**m**	man
f	fun	**k**	king	**n**	noon

r   room (r is always pronounced in Arabic regardless of its position in the word.)

s	say	**t**	ten	**y**	yes
sh	shine	**w**	well	**z**	zero

Please note that there are no **p** or **v** sounds in Arabic. Small **p** is usually replaced by **b** as in bansyoun for pension, and **v** is replaced by **f** as in karnafaal for carnival.

The Arabic consonants represented by the capital letters **S**, **D**, **T**, **Z** are vocal versions of **s**, **d**, **t**, **z**. You need to open your mouth as if you are saying **aah** and make the sound at the back of your mouth.

S   SabaaH = morning   **T**   Tayyib = O.K.
D   beiD = eggs   **Z**   Zareef = charming

'   This sound is usually called a glottal stop. It is similar to the sound produced if you try to say butter or bottle without the **tt**, as in Cockney.

The following Arabic consonants have no equivalent in English:

H   as in the Arabic *H*agz (reservation).

To produce this sound you have to constrict the back of the throat and breathe out heavily, like a deep sigh.

kh   as in the Arabic *kh*amsa (five).

The **kh** in Arabic is similar to the final sound in the Scottish word lo*ch*.

gh   as in the Arabic *gh*aali (expensive)

The **gh** in Arabic is similar to the strongly pronounced French **r** in **merci**.

Ɛ   as in the Arabic *Ɛ*arabi (Arab, Arabic)

The **Ɛ** sound in Arabic is like a violent glottal stop '.

q   as in the Arabic *q*ur'aan (Qu'ran)

The **q** in Arabic is similar to **k** but produced further back in the mouth. It is used very rarely in colloquial Egyptian.

Double consonants
Arabic consonants may also be doubled. Double consonants are pronounced like double sounds in English words, e.g. u*nn*erve, di*ss*atisfied, and i*rr*egular; and in the following Arabic words: hu*ww*a (he), hi*yy*a (she).

Pronunciation in connected speech
Vowel sounds are lost when they have other vowel sounds before or after them. For example:

li *i*lbint	*lil* bint	(for the girl)
fi *i*lmatHaf	*fil* matHaf	(in the museum)

Stress
There are two places for the stress in colloquial Arabic:
1) The last syllable but one, as in:
   taz*k*ara (ticket) **mu*ha*ndis** (engineer/architect) **fa*laa*fil** (bean burgers)
2) The last syllable, if it has a long vowel, as in:
   ilfu*loos* (money) **ikki*beer*** (the big)

INTRODUCTIONS AND GREETINGS

Arrival When arriving at an airport (or a sea port) you will find passport and customs procedures standard and easy to follow. Port officers are helpful and they usually guide the passengers to passport and customs counters. Information is usually given in English and Arabic on well-positioned boards. Always look for:

Arrival	**wuSool**	وصول
Exit	**khuroog**	خروج
Customs	**ilgumruk**	الجمرك
Passports	**ilgawazaat**	الجوازات

Points to remember Before setting out on your journey check your duty-free allowances. Some Arab countries do not allow the import of alcoholic drinks, and others require the exchange of a certain amount of hard currency (pounds sterling or dollars) for local currency on arrival.

The weekend in most Arab countries is on Thursday and Friday (**ilkhamees wiggumɛa**). Friday for Muslims is the equivalent of Sunday for Christians.

ahlan wa sahlan/Hello

Bill Taylor and his colleague Catherine Evans are two young journalists travelling together. They arrive at Cairo airport in the morning. As they come out of the arrival hall, they see an Egyptian couple with a board showing their names. Bill approaches them.

Bill:	**SabaaH ilkheir**, 'ana Bill Taylor wi di zmilti Catherine Evans.
Kamaal:	**'ahlan wa sahlan**, 'ana Kamaal salem, wi di zugti Nadya.
Bill &	
Catherine:	'ahlan wa sahlan, **furSa saɛeeda**.
Nadya:	**'irriHla kaanit kwayyisa?**
Catherine:	**'aywa, irriHla kaanit kwayyisa giddan.**
Kamaal:	**'ishshunaT fein?**

Bill:	**'ishshunaT ahih.**
Kamaal:	**Tayyib, itfaDDalu, 'ilɛarabiyya fil maw'af.**
Catherine:	**shukran, huwwal huteil biɛeed?**
Nadya:	**la' ilhuteil 'urayyib, mish biɛeed, laakin ishshunaT ti'eela.**
Bill:	'aywa. 'ishshunaT ti'eela giddan.
Kamaal:	Tayyib, itfaDDalu.

Words and phrases from the dialogue

SabaaH ilkheir	Good morning
'ana Bill Taylor	*I am* Bill Taylor
wi di zmilti/zugti	*and this is* my colleague/wife
'ahlan wa sahlan	Hello
furSa saɛeeda	pleased to meet you
'irriHla kaanit kwayyisa?	*Was the flight* good?
'aywa	Yes
'irriHla kaanit kwayyisa giddan	*the flight was* very good
'ishshunaT *fein?*	*Where are* the suitcases?
'ishshunaT *ahih*	The suitcases *are here*
Tayyib	All right, O.K.
itfaDDalu	Let's go
'ilɛarabiyya fil maw'af	*The car* is in the car park
shukran	Thank you
huwwal huteil *biɛeed?*	Is the hotel *far away?*
la' ilhuteil *'urayyib*	No, the hotel is *nearby*
mish biɛeed	*not* far
laakin	but
'ishshunaT *ti'eela*	the suitcases are *heavy*

Introductions

In Arab countries people usually shake hands when they meet and when they say goodbye.

'ana Bill	I am Bill
wi di zmilti (zimilti)	and this is my (female) colleague
wi da zmileeli (zimeeli)	and this is my (male) colleague
wi di zugti	and this is my wife
wi da zougi	and this is my husband

Greetings

SabaaH *ilkheir/innoor*	*good* morning.
masaa' *ilkheir/innoor*	*good* afternoon/evening
ahlan wa sahlan	Hello/How do you do?
ahlan	Hello/How do you do?
marHab/marHaba	Hello/How do you do?
furSa saɛeeda	Pleased to meet you.

SabaaH innoor and masaa'innoor mean 'Good morning' and 'Good evening' respectively but they are normally used as responses rather than to initiate greetings.

Polite expressions

Tayyib	Well! All right
itfaDDalu	let's go/after you (pl.)
shukran	thanks/thank you
min faDlak/faDlik	please (m./f.)
'aywa	yes
la'	no

itfaDDalu is used in many situations and can also mean 'please go ahead' or 'here you are'.

Other useful expressions

irriHla kaanit?	The flight was . . ./Was the flight . . ?
kwayyis/kwayyisa	good, fine (m./f.)
kwayyis giddan	very good
fein . . ?	Where is/are . . ?

the way it works

Masculine and feminine

Words in Arabic are classified as nouns, verbs or prepositions. Nouns and verbs have masculine and feminine forms. In colloquial Arabic some nouns can be made feminine by adding the sound **a** to the end of the masculine form.

Examples

Masculine	Feminine	Meaning
zimeel	zimeela	colleague (noun)
zoug	zouga	spouse (noun)
kwayyis	kwayyisa	good (adj.)
saɛeed	saɛeeda	pleased/happy (adj.)

Verbs have masculine and feminine forms for the singular, but only one form for the plural.

Examples

kaan	he was (m. sing.)	**kaanu**	they were (m. and f. pl.)
kaanit	she was (f. pl.)		

The definite article

il is the definite article in Arabic, like 'the' in English. The **l** sound in **il** disappears in some cases, and the first letter in the word is doubled instead.

Examples

huteil	hotel	**ilhuteil**	the hotel
ɛarabiyya	car	**ilɛarabiyya**	the car

maw'af	car park	ilmaw'af	the car park
*ri*Hla	flight	*irri*Hla	the flight
*shu*naT	suitcases	*ishshu*naT	the suitcases

I am . . . and This is . . .

The Arabic for 'I am Bill' is **'ana Bill**. (I/me Bill). The equivalent of the verb to be (am, is, are) in Arabic is not used in such structures as I am, he is, they are, this is, that is, etc. More examples are given below with their English translation.

'ana Bill	I Bill	I am Bill
'ana Catherine	I Catherine	I am Catherine
da zmeeli	This my colleague	This is my colleague (he)
di zugti	This my wife	This is my wife (she)
ilɛarabiyya fil maw'af	The car in the car park	The car is in the car park (it)
ishshunaT ti'eela	The suitcases heavy	The suitcases are heavy (they)

My

To say 'my' in Arabic you add **i** sound at the end of the noun, whether it is masculine or feminine, singular or plural. But when the noun has a feminine ending with an **a** sound, the pronunciation of the word changes and **ti** replaces the **a**.

Examples

zoug	husband	**zougi**	my husband
zouga	wife	**zugti**	my wife
zimeel	colleague	**zimeeli**	my colleague (m.)
zimeela	colleague	**zimilti**	my colleague (f.)
shunaT	suitcases	**shunaTi**	my suitcases
ɛarabiyya	car	**ɛarabiyyiti**	my car

things to do

1.1 Say the following in Arabic.

1 Hello!
2 Pleased to meet you.
3 I am Sally.
4 This is my colleague Tom.
5 I am Ahmad.
6 This is my wife Nadya.
7 Was the flight all right?
8 Yes, it was a very good flight.
9 Where is the car?
10 The car is in the car park.

BOOKING HOTEL ACCOMMODATION

Accommodation There are two main types of accommodation for people on holidays or business for a short period: hotels with star rating, and boarding houses called **bansyoun**. Guests in both types are always asked to fill in registration forms on arrival, giving passport details. There are also Youth Hostels in the big cities like Cairo, Alexandria, Luxor and Aswan.

Look for the following signs

Hotel	**funduq**	فندق
Boarding House/Pension	**bansyoun**	بنسيون
Youth Hostel	**beit shabaab**	بيت شباب
Reception	**'istiqbaal**	استقبال

Prices are fixed in hotels and Youth Hostels, but subject to negotiation in boarding houses.

'ana ɛandi Hagz/I have a reservation

Catherine:	masaa' ilkheir.
Receptionist:	masaa' innoor, **ayyi khidma?**
Catherine:	**'ana ɛandi Hagz hina.**
Receptionist:	**'il'ism min faDlik?**
Catherine:	**'ana 'ismi** Catherine Evans.
Receptionist:	**kaam leila?**
Catherine:	**talat layaali.**
Receptionist:	**'aywa feeh Hagz bismik**.

Catherine:	**feeh Hammaam wi tilifoun fil 'ouDa?**
Receptionist:	'aywa feeh, **'ouDa nimra khamsa, bi Hammaam wi tilifoun.**
Catherine:	shukran.
Receptionist:	**'ilmuftaaH ahuh,** 'itfaDDali.
Catherine:	shukran, **tiSbaH ɛala kheir.**

Words and phrases from the dialogue

'ayyi khidma	What can I do for you?
'ana ɛandi Hagz hina	I have a reservation here
'il'ism. min faDlik	What is the name, please?
'ana 'ismi	My name is
kaam leila?	How many nights?
talat layaali	3 nights
feeh Hagz bismik	There is a reservation in your name
feeh Hammaam	Is there a bathroom
wi tilifoun	and a telephone
fil 'ouDa?	in the room?
'ouDa nimra khamsa	Room No. 5
bi Hammaam wi tilifoun	with bathroom and telephone
'ilmuftaaH ahuh	Here is the key
tiSbaH ɛala kheir	Good night

ɛandak 'ouDa faDya?/Do you have a vacant room?

Bill:	massa' ilkheir.
Receptionist:	masaa' innoor, 'ayyi khidma?
Bill:	**ɛandak 'ouDa faDya** min faDlak?
Receptionist:	kaam leila?
Bill:	**'arbaɛ layaali** min faDlak.
Receptionist:	'aywa ɛandi.
Bill:	**'ana ɛaayiz 'ouDa-b Hammaam** wi tilifoun. **bi kaam?**
Receptionist:	**bikhamseen gineih fil youm, bil fiTaar.**
Bill:	Tayyib, kwayyis.
Receptionist:	'ouDa **nimra talaata.** ilmuftaaH ahuh, 'itfaDDal.
Bill:	shukran, **'ilfiTaar issaaɛa kaam?**
Receptionist:	**'ilfiTaar issaaɛa sabɛa.**
Bill:	Tayyib tiSbaH ɛala kheir.

Words and phrases from the dialogue

εandak 'ouDa faDya	do you have a vacant room?
'arbaε layaali	4 nights
εandi	I have
'ana εaayiz	I would like (want)
'ouDa-b Hammam	a room with ensuite bathroom
bi kaam?	what is the price?
bikhamseen gineih	50 pounds
fil youm	per day
bil fiTaar	including breakfast
nimra talaata	number 3
'ilfiTaar issaaεa kaam?	what time is breakfast?
'ilfiTaar issaaεa sabεa	breakfast is at 7 o'clock

Polite expressions

'ayyi khidma?	what can I do for you?
tiSbaH εala kheir	good night (to a male)
tiSbaHi εala kheir	good night (to a female)
tiSbaHu εala kheir	good night (to more than one, male or female)
'itfaDDal/'itfaDDali	here you are (m./f.)

Other useful words and phrases

'ouDa bisreer waaHid	a single room
'ouDa bisrirein (Dabil)	a twin bedroom (double)
'ouDa-b dushsh	a room with a shower
likaam shakhS?	for how many persons?
'ilmaTεam	the restaurant
hinaak	there
lishakhS waaHid	for one person (single)
mumkin tiktib/tiktibi ilHisaab (ilfatoora)?	Would you like to write (m./f.) the bill?
mumkin 'ashoof ?	can I see?
ilgawaaz/ilbasbour	the passport

the way it works

Personal pronouns

'ana = I	'iHna = we
'inta = you·(m.)	'intu = you (pl.)
'inti = you (f.)	humma = they
huwwa = he	
hiyya = she	

I have, you have, he has, etc.

To say 'I have' in Arabic you add the relevant end pronoun to the word εand which means 'possess', as in column 1 below. Personal pronouns can also be used, as in column 2.

εandi	'ana εeandi	I have
εandak	'inta εandak	you have (m. s.)
εandik	'inti εandik	you have (f. s.)
εandu	huwwa εandu	he (it) has
εandaha	hiyya εandaha	she (it) has
εandina	'iHna εandina	we have
εanduku	'intu εanduku	you have (pl.)
εanduhum	humma εanduhum	they have

Examples

εandak Hagz?	do you have a reservation?
'aywa εandi Hagz	yes, I have a reservation
εandina Hagz	We have a reservation

Possessive pronouns

To say 'my/your/his', etc. in Arabic, you add the relevant ending to the noun:

Masculine nouns		**Feminine nouns**	
Arabic	*English*	*Arabic*	*English*
ismi	my name	zugti	my wife
ismak	your name (m. s.)	zugtak	your wife (m. s.)
ismik	your name (f. s.)	zimiltik	your colleague (f. s.)
ismu	his (its) name	zugtu	his wife
ismaha	her (its) name	zimilitha	her colleague

The preposition bi

The Arabic preposition **bi** is mostly used to mean 'with' as in **bi Hammaam** (with bathroom). It also means 'in' as in **bismi** (in my name), or 'for' as in **bi kaam** (for how much). **bi** loses the **i** sound when it is followed or preceded by a vowel.

Examples

'ouDa-b Hammaam	room with a bathroom
'ouDa-b dushsh	room with a shower
bil fiTaar	with (including) breakfast
'ilHagz bismi	the reservation is in my name
Hagz bism Bill Taylor	reservation in Bill Taylor's name
bi kaam il'ouDa?	(for) how much is the room?
bi khamseen gineih fil leila	(for) fifty pounds per night

Numerals 1–10

There are two forms of cardinal numbers from 1–10 in colloquial Arabic. One form is used for numbering, telling the time, ordering food or drinks, and talking about money (1), and the other form is used for counting objects or people (2).

(1)	Meaning	(2)
waaHid/waHda	1. one m/f	**waaHid/waHda**
itnein	2. two	**itnein**
talaata	3. three	**talat**
arbaεa	4. four	**arbaε**
khamsa	5. five	**khamas**
sitta	6. six	**sitt**
sabεa	7. seven	**sabaε**
tamanya	8. eight	**taman**
tisεa	9. nine	**tisaε**
εashara	10. ten	**εashar**

Examples

nimra talaata	No. 3	**talat layaali**	3 nights
nimra khamsa	No. 5	**arbaε layaali**	4 nights
issaaεa sitta	6 o'clock	**sitt shunaT**	6 suitcases

From 11 onwards, one form of cardinal numbers is used for all purposes.

More will be said about numerals later.

A list of cardinal and ordinal numbers is given in the vocabulary at the end of this book, p. 79.

things to do

1.2 You are Bill Taylor. You are checking in at a hotel in Cairo. Practise saying the following in Arabic, to a female receptionist.

1 I have a reservation here.
2 My name is Bill Taylor.
3 I would like a room with a shower, please.
4 How much is it per night?
5 Where is the restaurant, please?

1.3 You are Fay Wilson. You are booking a room in a hotel. Practise saying the following in Arabic, to a male receptionist.

1 Do you have a vacant room?
2 No, I would like a room with a bathroom.
3 Four nights, please.
4 Can I have the key, please?
5 Where is the room, please?

ORDERING FOOD AND DRINK

ilfiTaar fil huteil/
Breakfast at the hotel

Mr and Mrs Clark are a middle-aged couple on holiday in Egypt. They are sitting in the hotel restaurant waiting to order their breakfast.

Waiter:	SabaH ilkheir. **taklu 'eih yafandim?**
Mr Clark:	SabaaH ilkheir. **ɛandak 'eih?**
Waiter:	**ɛandi** fool, wi beiD, wi gibna, wimrabba.
Mrs Clark:	**'ana 'aakhud** gibna-w beiD. **feeh ɛeish?**
Waiter:	**feeh** ɛeish yamadaam.
Mr Clark:	feeh mirabbit 'eih?
Waiter:	feeh mirabbit balaH wi-mrabbit teen.
Mr Clark:	'ana 'aakhud fool wi-mrabbit balaH, wi ɛeish **Tabɛan**.
Waiter:	**HaaDir yamadaam. tishrabu 'eih? 'ahwa, shaay, ɛaSeer?**
Mrs Clark:	**'ana 'ashrab shaay bi laban.**
Mr Clark:	wana 'ashrab 'ahwa-b laban.
Waiter:	**'ayyi khidma. 'ouDa nimra kaam?**
Mrs Clark:	nimra khamsa-w talateen.

Words and phrases from the dialogue

taklu 'eih?	What would you like to eat?
yafandim/yamadaam	Sir/Madam
ɛandak 'eih?	What have you got?
ɛandi	I have/There is
'ana 'aakhud	I'll have
feeh ɛeish?	Is there bread?
feeh	There is
Tabɛan	of course

HaaDir yamadaam	Yes, Madam
tishrabu 'eih?	What would you like to drink?
a'hwa shaay, ɛaSeer?	Coffee, tea, fruit juice?
'ana 'ashrab (shaay)	I'll have (tea)
shaay *bi laban*	tea *with milk*
'ahwa-*b laban*	coffee *with milk*
'ayyi khidma.	certainly/at your service
'ouDa nimra kaam?	(What) room number?

Polite expressions

'ayyi khidma.	Certainly, at your service.
yafandim	Sir/Madam is a polite form of address for men and women.
winta **yafandim**	*And you*, Sir.
wi HaDritak **yafandim**	*And you*, Sir. (more polite)
winti **ya madaam**	*And you*, Madam.
wi HaDritik **ya madaam**	*And you*, Madam. (more polite)

ya is used before a name or form of address when talking to or calling someone. Other forms of address for men are: **sayyid**, **beih**, **'ustaaz**, **sheikh**. Other forms of address for women are: **sitt**, **haanim**.

Food and drinks

fool	Broad beans cooked in water until soft and brown and served with oil (or butter) and salt. Also known as **fool midammis**

beiD	eggs	**mirabbit farawla**	strawberry jam
beiDa	one egg	**ɛeish**	bread
gibna	cheese	**ɛeish baladi**	local (flat) bread
gibna beiDa	white cheese	**ɛeish feenu**	french bread
gibna roomi	romano cheese	**shaay bilaban**	tea with milk
mirabba	jam	**'ahwa-b laban**	coffee with milk
mirabbit balaH/teen	date/fig jam	**ɛaSeer**	fruit juice
zibna	butter		

the way it works

The present tense

Verbs in the present tense with I and you are formed like this:

Person		take	eat	drink
I (m. & f.)	ana	**'aakhud**	**'aakul**	**'ashrab**
You (m.)	inta	**taakhud**	**taakul**	**tishrab**
You (f.)	inti	**takhdi**	**takli**	**tishrabi**
We (m. & f.)	iHna	**naakhud**	**naakul**	**nishrab**
You (pl.)	intu	**takhdu**	**taklu**	**tishrabu**

17

What would you like to have?

There are three ways of asking this question in Arabic. Like English you can ask:

1. What would you like to have? **taakhud 'eih?** (m.)
   takhdi 'eih (f.)

   The answer would be, e.g. **'aakhud shaay** (I would like tea) or **'aakhud gibna-w beiD** (I would like cheese and eggs).

2. What would you like to eat? **taakul 'eih?** (m.)
   takli 'eih? (f.)

   The answer would be, e.g. **'aakul gibna-w beiD** (I would like to eat cheese and eggs).

3. What would you like to drink? **tishrab 'eih?** (m.)
   tishrabi 'eih? (f.)

   The answer would be, e.g. **'ashrab shaay** (I would like to drink tea).

Mirabba and **mirabbit**
The word **mirabba** means 'jam'. To say a particular kind of jam, such as date jam, you have to use the form **mirabbit** so you have **mirabbit balaH** (date jam), **mirabbit teen** (fig jam), or **mirabbit farawla** (strawberry jam).

Pronunciation of wi and bi

These prepositions lose the sound **i** when they are used before or after a vowel.

Examples
'aakhud gibna-w beiD	(wi beiD)
nimra khamsa-w talateen	(wi talateen)
'ashrab 'ahwa-b laban	(bi laban)
'aakhud fool wi beiD	I'll take beans and eggs
'aakhud gibna-w beiD	I'll have cheese and eggs
ashrab shaay bi laban	I'll have tea with milk
ashrab ahwa-b laban	I'll have coffee with milk

things to do

2.1 Say the following in Arabic

Ask the waiter	1	What have you got?
	2	What jam have you got?
Ask your friend Sarah	3	Would you like to have tea?
	4	Would you like to have juice?
Ask your friend Karim	5	What would you like to eat?
	6	What would you like to drink?
Say	7	I would like to have beans, cheese and date jam.
	8	I would like to have coffee with milk.

REFRESHMENTS

Tea, coffee, cold drinks and snacks are available in cafés, shops and restaurants, particularly in tourist areas. Cold drinks are available everywhere. There is always a stall round the corner selling fizzy drinks and bottled water, even if there is no café or grocer's nearby:

Bill and Catherine stop at a café in **khaan ilkhalili** for refreshments.

fil 'ahwa/At the café

Bill:	massa' ilkheir.
Waiter:	**masaa' innoor. 'ahlan wasahlan.**
Bill:	**ɛayzeen sandwitshaat, ɛandak 'eih?**
Waiter:	ɛandi fool wi **falaafil** wi gibna-w beiD.
Bill:	'itnein fool witnein falaafil min faDlak.
Catherine:	**ɛandak Haaga sa'ɛa?**
Waiter:	ɛandi bibsi-w kuka koula-w teem wi ɛaSeer.
Bill:	**feeh beera?**
Waiter:	**la' mafeesh beera, 'aasif.**
Catherine:	**feeh ɛaSeer 'eih?**
Waiter:	**feeh ɛaSeer manga-w ɛaSeer gawaafa.**
Catherine:	'ana aakhud ɛaSeer manga min faDlak.
Bill:	wana aakhud bibsi min faDlak.
Waiter:	HaaDir. 'ayyi khidma.

19

Words and phrases from the dialogue

masaa' innoor	Good evening!
ɛayzeen sandwitshaat	We would like some sandwiches.
ɛandak 'eih?	What have you got?
falaafil	Bean burgers.
ɛandak Haaga sa'ɛa?	Have you got any cold drinks?
ɛandi bibsi-w	I have Pepsi and
kuka-koula-w	Coca-Cola and
teem	Team (fizzy lemon drink)
wi ɛaSeer	and juice (fruit juices)
feeh beera?	Is there beer?/Do you sell beer?
la' mafeesh beera.	No, there's no beer.
'aasif	Sorry
feeh ɛaSeer 'eih?	What juices have you got?
ɛaSeer manga-w	Mango juice and
ɛaSeer gawaafa.	Guava juice.

Useful words and phrases

Fruit juices

ɛaSeer	juice
ɛaSeer burtu'aan	orange juice
ɛaSeer lamoon	lemon juice
ɛaSeer farawla	strawberry juice
ɛaSeer mouz	banana juice
ɛaSeer TamaaTim	tomato juice
ɛaSeer 'aSab	sugar cane juice

Hot and Cold

'il bibsi di sa'ɛa	This Pepsi is cold
'il bibsi di sukhna (mish sa'ca)	This Pepsi is hot (not cold)
'il 'akl da sukhn	This food is hot
'il 'akl da baarid	This food is cold

Salt and sugar

bi malH	with salt	bi sukkar	with sugar
bi malH 'aleel	with little salt	bi sukkar 'aleel	with little sugar
bidoon malH	without salt	bidoon sukkar	without sugar

the way it works

Would like

ɛayzeen, is the plural of ɛaayiz (m) and ɛayza (f) which means 'would like'.

Examples

'ana ɛaayiz sandwitsh	I would like a sandwich
Magda ɛayza bibsi	Magda would like Pepsi
'iHna ɛayzeen ɛaSeer	We would like juice

Using numbers when ordering

When ordering food or drinks use the same form of cardinal numbers as used for numbering. (See p. 79 at the end of the book.)

Examples

'itnein (sandwitsh) fool	two bean sandwiches
talaata falaafil	three falaafil sandwiches
'arbaɛa gibna	four cheese sandwiches
khamsa manga	five mango juice drinks
waaHid bibsi	one Pepsi

Note that, like English, the word 'sandwiches' can also be repeated when giving an order. **'itnein fool** or **'itnein sandwitsh fool**.

things to do

2.2   Order these food and drinks:

1   Three falaafil sandwiches
2   Two cheese sandwiches
3   Four orange juice drinks
4   One bean sandwich
5   Six Pepsis
6   Five lemon juice drinks

CHANGING MONEY

You can easily change money at banks. There are branches of the major national and foreign banks in airports and the larger cities. Banks usually give a better rate than exchange booths, hotels, or shops.

ATMs are also a convenient way to withdraw money while traveling in Egypt, as well as some other Arab countries.

The Egyptian currency is called **gineih**, usually known in English as 'Egyptian pound'. A **gineih** is 100 **piastres**. A piastre is known as **'irsh**, and the plural is **'uroosh**.

| gineih | Egyptian pound | جنيه |
| **meet 'irsh** | 100 piastres | ١٠٠ قرش |

Arab currencies are shown in a table at the end of this book (p. 91).

Look for the following signs:

		بنك
Bank	**bank**	مصرف
	maSrif	
Bureau de change	**taghyeer ilɛumla**	تغيير العملة
	Siraafa	صرافة
Cash desk	**ilkhazeena**	الخزينة

Fil bank/At the bank

Catherine:	il'istirleeni-b kaam, min faDlak?
Clerk:	bikhamsa gneih wi talateen 'irsh.
Catherine:	widdulaar bi Kaam?
Clerk:	iddulaar bitnein gineih wi nuSS.
Catherine:	Tayyib. aghayyar miyya stirleeni, wimiyya-w talateen dulaar.
Clerk:	'ayyi khidma, mumkin ashoof ilbasbour?
Catherine:	'aywa. itfaDDal.
Clerk:	Tayyib imli listimaara di, wimDi hina, min faDlik.
Catherine:	HaaDir. ilfuloos minein?
Clerk:	ilfuloos min ilkhazeena, hinaak.

Words and phrases from the dialogue

il'istirleeni-b kaam?	How much is the pound sterling?
bikhamsa gneih	for five pounds
wi talateen 'irsh	and thirty-five piastres
widdulaar bi Kaam?	And how much is the dollar?
bitnein gineih wi nuSS	two pounds and fifty piastres (or a half)
aghayyar miyya stirleeni	I'll change one hundred pounds sterling
wimiyya-w talateen dulaar	and one hundred and thirty dollars
mumkin ashoof ilbasbour?	Can I see your passport?
imli listimaara di	Fill in this form
wimDi hina	and sign here
ilfuloos minein?	Where do I collect the money (cash)?
min ilkhazeena	from the cash desk

Useful words and phrases

gineih/ginihaat	pound/pounds
gineih istirleeni	pound sterling
gineih maSri	Egyptian pound
'irsh/'uroosh	piastre/piastres
dulaar/dularaat	dollar/dollars
sheek/shikaat	cheque/cheques

23

sheek siyaaHi	traveller's cheque
sheekat siyaaHiyya	traveller's cheques
istimara	form
mumkin aghayyar?	Can I change?
ɛaayiz (ɛayza) aghayyar	I would like to change
ɛaayiz tighayyar kaam?	How much do you want to change?

the way it works

Pronunciation

The following are further examples of the loss of **i** in il, bi, wi, gineih, and istirleeni, when these sounds are followed or preceded by other vowels:

il'istirleeni-**b k**aam?	**bi k**aam
miyy**a s**tirleen	miyya **is**tirleeni
wi miyya-**w** talateen dulaar	wi talateen dulaar
imli **l**istimaara di (f.)	imli i**l**istimaara di
iml**a l**istimaara di (m).	iml**a** i**l**istimaara di
bikhams**a g**neih	bikhams**a g**ineih

More about numerals

The form of numerals used for numbering, ordering food and drinks and telling the time is also used for talking about sums of money (see p. 79, column 1). Please note that there are two forms for the number 'one' **waaHid** (masculine) and **waHda** (feminine) although neither of these forms are used when talking about money, except for emphasis. When talking about money you say the following:

gineih or **gineih waaHid** (m.)	one pound
lira or **lira waHda** (f.)	one lira
itnein gineih/lira/dulaar*	two pounds/lira/dollars
talaata gneih/lira/dulaar	three pounds/lira/dollars
'arbaɛa gneih/lira/dulaar	four pounds/lira/dollars
khamsa gneih/lira/dulaar	five pounds/lira/dollars

sitta gneih/lira/dulaar	six pounds/lira/dollars
sabɛa gneih/lira/dulaar	seven pounds/lira/dollars
tamanya gneih/lira/dulaar	eight pounds/lira/dollars
tisɛa gneih/lira/dulaar	nine pounds/lira/dollars
ɛashara gneih/lira/dulaar	ten pounds/lira/dollars

*Notice that the object counted is in the singular.

From **HiDaashar** (eleven) onwards the same form of cardinal numerals is used for the hours, money and all other objects counted. The number is followed by the noun in the singular in all cases. When telling the time, the number comes after the word for hour. See p. 79 at the end of this book for a list of these numerals.

things to do

2.3 You are trying to change some foreign money for Egyptian pounds. Say the following in Arabic:

1 Can I change pounds sterling here?
2 How much is a pound sterling?
3 Can I change traveller's cheques?
4 No, dollars.
5 One hundred and thirty-two dollars.

2.4 You are Michael. You are having a conversation with your hotel manager in the Sudan. What do you say?

1	Michael:	Ask about the number of the rooms in the hotel.
2	Manager:	Feeh khamsa-w sitteen 'ouDa.
3	Michael:	Ask how much a single room is.
4	Manager:	khamsa warbiɛeen gineih filleila.
5	Michael:	Ask if there is a bank in the hotel.
6	Manager:	'aywa feeh.
7	Michael:	Ask if you can change money here.
8	Manager:	ɛaayiz tighayyar 'ɛih?
9	Michael:	Say you would like to change dollars.
10	Manager:	Tabɛan mumkin.

TELLING THE TIME

issaaɛa kaam?/What time is it?

Bill is asking about the times of meals at the hotel.

Bill:	**'ilfiTaar issaaɛa kaam**, min faDlak?
Receptionist:	min issaaɛa sabɛa lissaaɛa tisɛa.
Bill:	**wilɛasha-s saaɛa kaam?**
Receptionist:	ilɛasha **min issaaɛa sabɛa-w nuSS lissaaɛa ɛashara.**
Bill:	**issaaɛa kaam dilwa'ti?**
Receptionist:	issaaɛa dilwa'ti sabɛalla rubɛ.
Bill:	**il'akhbaar issaaɛa kaam firradyu?**
Receptionist:	il'akhbaar **issaaɛa tamanya-w nuSS.**
Bill:	Tayyib. **'arooH atɛashsha 'awwalan, wibaɛdein** asmaɛ il'akhbaar. **tiSbaH ɛala kheir.**
Receptionist:	tisbaH ɛala kheir yafandim.

Words and phrases from the dialogue

'ilfiTaar issaaɛa kaam?	What time is breakfast?
wilɛasha-s saaɛa kaam?	And what time is supper?
min issaaɛas sabɛa-w nuss	from half past seven
lissaaɛa ɛashara	to ten o'clock
'issaaɛa kaam dilwa'ti?	What time is it now?

il'akhbaar issaaɛa kaam?	What time is the news?
firradyu	on the radio
issaaɛa tamanya-w nuSS	at half past eight
'arooH	I'll go
atɛashsha 'awwalan	and have supper first
wibaɛdein	and then (and after that)
asmaɛ il'akhbaar	I'll listen to the news

Useful words and phrases

'ilfiTaar	breakfast
'ilghada	lunch
'ilɛasha	supper/dinner

Sequence of events

awwalan	first
'arooH atɛashsha awwalan	I'll go and have supper first
wibaɛdein	then/later
wibaɛdein asmaɛ il'akhbaar	then I'll listen to the news

Verbs with different persons

person		listen	go	have breakfast	have lunch	have supper
I	'ana	asmaɛ	arooH	afTar	atghadda	atɛashsha
You (m.)	'inta	tismaɛ	tirooH	tifTar	titghadda	titɛashsha
You (f.)	'inti	tismaɛi	tirooHi	tifTari	titghaddi	titɛashshi
He	huwwa	yismaɛ	yirooH	yifTar	yitghadda	yitɛashsha
She	hiyya	tismaɛ	tirooH	tifTar	titghadda	titɛashsha
We	'iHna	nismaɛ	nirooH	nifTar	nitghadda	nitɛashsha
You (pl.)	'intu	tismaɛu	tirooHu	tifTaru	titghaddu	titɛashshu

Telling the time

The numerals used for telling the time are the same as those used for sums of money and ordering food and drinks. But note that the word **issaaɛa** (o'clock) is said before the number (see p. 26 above, and p. 79 for a list of cardinal numbers).

To tell the time, say the hour first, then **illa** if it is something *to* the hour, or **wi** if it is something *past* the hour.

Examples

issaaɛa sitta	It is six o'clock
issaaɛa dilwa'ti talaata	It (the time) is now 3 o'clock
issaaɛa-rbaɛa	It is 4 o'clock
issaaɛa khamsa-w ɛashara	It is ten past five
issaaɛa-rbaɛa-**lla** rubɛ	It is quarter to four
issaaɛa-tnein **wi** nuSS	It is half past two
issaaɛa talaata-**w** nuSS	It is half past three

issaaɛa-HDaashar **wi** rubɛ	It is quarter past eleven
issaaɛa-tnaashar **illa** khamsa	It is five minutes to twelve
issaaɛa waHda-**lla** rubɛ	It is quarter to one

Note the loss of **a** in **arbaɛa**, the loss of **i** in **wi** and the loss of **i** in **illa** because of the **a** sound that precedes them.

things to do

2.5 Ask the following questions and reply using the clock and watch faces shown:

1 What time is breakfast?
2

7 What time is it now?
8

3 What time is the news?
4

9 Is it quarter to eight now?
10 No it is 8.15.

5 What time can I have supper?
6

FINDING YOUR WAY

feeh maktab bareed 'urayyib?/Is there a post office nearby?

Catherine is asking a shop assistant if there is a post office nearby.

Catherine: **feeh maktab bareed 'urayyib min hina?**
Assistant: 'aywa feeh. **fi shaariɛ ilbustaan.**
Catherine: **'arooH izzaay** min faDlik?
Assistant: **imshi ɛala Tool li 'aakhir ishshaariɛ da**. wibaɛdein **Hawwidi shmaal**.
Catherine: Tayyib. 'amshi-l 'aakhir ishshaariɛ waHawwid shimaal. wibaɛdein?
Assistant: imshi ɛala Tool. **taani shaariɛ shimaal** huwwa shaariɛ ilbustaan.
Catherine: wi maktab ilbareed fi shaariɛ ilbustan?
Assistant: 'aywa **taalit mabna ɛala-l yimeen**.
Catherine: shukran.
Assistant: **ilɛafw** yafandim. 'ayyi khidma.

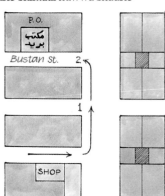

Words and phrases from the dialogue

feeh maktab bareed 'urayyib min hina?	is there a post office nearby?
fi shaariɛ ilbustaan	in Bustan street
'arooH izzaay?	how do I get there?
imshi *ɛala Tool*	walk *straight on*
li'aakhir **ishshariɛ da**	*to the end* of this street
Hawwidi **shmaal**	*turn* left
taani **shaarɛ shimaal**	*the second* street left
huwwa	it is
taalit **mabna**	*the third* building
ɛala-l *yimeen*	on the *right*
'ilɛafw	it's a pleasure/all right

fein 'a'rab bi'aala?/ Where is the nearest grocery?

Bill is asking one of the passers-by about the nearest grocery.

Bill: **fein 'a'rab bi'aala** min faDlak?
Passer-by: **'awwil shaariɛ yimeen**. ilbi'aala **raabiɛ dukkan ɛalash-shimaal.**
Bill: **shukran ya sayyid.**
Passer-by: **ilɛafw.** 'ayyi khidma.

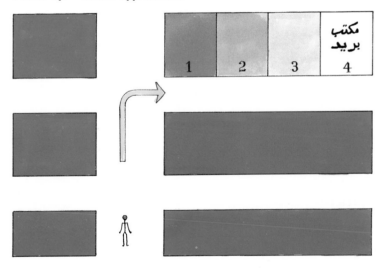

Words and phrases from the dialogue

fein 'a'rab bi'aala?	where is the nearest grocery?
'awwil shaariɛ yimeen	the first street on the right
raabiɛ dukkan	the fourth shop
ɛalash-shimaal	on the left

Polite expressions

shukran yasayyid	thank you, sir
ilɛafw	it is a pleasure/that is all right

Useful words and phrases

feeh 'ahwa ('agzakhana)?	is there a café (pharmacy)?
fittigaah	towards, in the direction of
fein ilmaHaTTa?	where is the station?
fein maHaTTit il'aTr?	where is the railway station?
fein ism ilbulees (ishshurTa)	where is the police station?
ɛandak khareeTit maSr?	do you have a map of Egypt?
'uddaam ilhuteil	in front of the hotel
wara-l gaamiɛ	behind the mosque
ganb il agzakhaana	beside the pharmacy
ɛala ymeen ilhuteil	to the right of the hotel
ɛala shmaal ilhuteil	to the left of the hotel
idkhul yimeen/shimaal	turn right/left
khud 'awwil shaariɛ yimeen	take/turn at the first street on the right
'imshi meet mitr ta'reeban	go/walk about 100 metres
'imshi-liHaad	go up to
ɛala-n naSya	at the corner
'aakhir ishshaariɛ	the end of the street/road
awwil ishshaariɛ	the beginning of the street
mumkin taakhud taksi	you can take a taxi
mumkin taakhud ilmitru	you can take the Metro
mumkin taakhud 'utubees	you can take a bus
laazim taakhud il'aTr	you have to take the train

Some useful words in Arabic

street	**shaariɛ**	police	**ishshurTa/ilbulees**
square	**midaan/saaHa**	police station	**'ism ilbulees**
post office	**maktab bareed**	station	**maHaTTa**
stationers	**maktaba**	café	**'ahwa**
pharmacy	**'agzakhaana**	museum	**matHaf**
pharmacy	**Saydaliyya**		

the way it works

Asking for directions

Here are 3 different ways of asking for directions:

feeh . . . ?	**fein . . . ?**	**'arooH . . . izzaay?**
Is there a . . . ?	Where is . . . ?	How do I get to . . . ?

Examples

(a)   **feeh bi'aala 'urayyiba min hina?** (f.)   Is there a grocery nearby?
        feeh maktab bareed 'urayyib min Is there a post office nearby?
        hina? (m.)

(b)   **fein ilmatHaf ilmaSri?**   Where is the Egyptian museum?
        fein 'ism ilbulees?   Where is the police station?

(c)   **'arooH ilmatHaf izzaay?**   How do I get to the museum?
        'arooH il'azhar izzaay?   How do I get to Azhar?
        εaayiz (εayza) arooH ilhuteil.   I would like to get to the hotel.

Giving directions

Special forms of verbs are used to give directions, as shown in the table below: one for talking to a singular masculine, one for talking to a singular feminine, and one for talking to plural masculine and feminine.

person	walk	take	go (turn) into	turn	cross
(m.)	'imshi	khud	'idkhul	Hawwid	εaddi
(f.)	'imshi	khudi	'idkhuli	Hawwidi	εaddi
(pl.)	'imshu	khudu	'idkhulu	Hawwidu	εaddu

Ordinal numbers (1–10)

These forms are used before masculine and feminine nouns.

Examples

awwil shaariε (m.)	first street	**saadis youm** (m.)	sixth day
taani mabna (m.)	second building	**saabiε 'ouDa** (f.)	seventh room
taalit leila (f.)	third night	**taamin mabna** (m.)	eighth building
raabiε dukkaan (m.)	fourth shop	**taasiε dour** (m.)	ninth floor
khaamis maHaTTa (f.)	fifth station	**εaashir maHatta** (f.)	tenth station

things to do

3.1   Ask for the following directions:

    1   Where is the nearest pharmacy?
    2   How can I get to the post office?

3 Where is the police station?
4 Is there a grocery nearby?
5 How do I get to the railway station?

3.2 Give directions to taxi drivers taking you to each of the places marked on the map below. Starting from your hotel (H) go to destinations 1, 2, 3, 4, and 5.

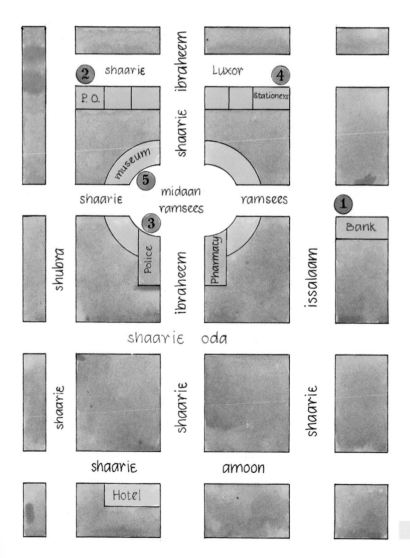

TRAVELLING BY BUS OR TAXI

All the cities in the Arab countries have bus services and taxis. There are also coach services that link cities, towns and villages, in addition to the railway networks, in some countries such as Egypt and Saudi Arabia. Taxis normally wait outside railway stations, airports, big hotels, and tourist sites. You can also hail a taxi in the street. It is not unusual to share a taxi with others already in it, or for the taxi to stop and take others on the way to your destination. However, you can have a taxi on your own if you want to, especially if it is a long distance, or if you have a lot of luggage. Taxis you can have on your own are called **limousine**, and in some countries you can also order them by phone. The other type of taxi is known as **sirfees** (service), or just **taksi** (taxi).

Signs to look for are:

Station	**maHaTTa**	محطة
Stop	**maw'af**	موقف
Bus	**'utubees**	أتوبيس
Taxicab	**taksi**	تاكسي

'utubees nimra kaam?/Which bus?

Bill and Catherine are going to see the pyramids in Giza and they want to go by bus. They ask their Egyptian friend how to get there.

Bill: 'iHna εayzeen nirooH ilharam, **naakhud 'utubees nimra kaam?**

Kamaal: **mafeesh 'utubees min hina lilharam. laazim tighayyaru-f baab ilHadeed.**

Catherine: naakhud nimra kaam min hina?

Kamaal: takhdu nimra siTTaashar min hina-l baab ilHadeed?

Bill: **wi baεdein nimra kaam** min baab ilHadeed.

Kamaal: wi baεdein takhdu nimra tisεa lilharam.

Bill: Tayyib, shukran.

Words and phrases from the dialogue

εayzeen nirooH ilharam	we want to go to the Pyramids
naakhud 'utubees nimra kaam?	which bus shall we take?
	bus number what shall we take?
mafeesh 'utubees min hina lilharam	there is no bus from here to the Pyramids
laazim tighayyaru-f baab ilHadeed	you have to change (buses) at baab El-Hadid
wi baεdein nimra kaam	then number what (bus)?

fil 'utubees/On the bus

Conductor: **tazaakir min faDlak.**

Bill: **'itnein baab ilHadeed**

Conductor: **tazkartein bikhamseen 'irsh. ittazkara-b khamsa-w εishreen 'irsh.**

Bill: 'itfaDDal. **aadi gneih wi haat ilbaa'i.**

Conductor: 'itfaDDal tazkartein, wilbaa'i khamseen 'irsh.

Bill: shukran

Conductor: 'ilεafw.

Words and phrases from the dialogue

tazaakir min faDlak	tickets please
'itnein baab ilHadeed	two (tickets) to Bab El-Hadid
tazkartein bikhamseen 'irsh	two tickets for fifty piastres
ittazkara-b khamsa-w εishreen 'irsh	twenty-five piastres for each (ticket)
'aadi gneih	here is a pound
wi haat ilbaa'i	and give me the change

'istiεmal ittaksi/Taking a taxi

Bill and Catherine decide after their outing to take a taxi back to the hotel.

Bill: (shouting)	taksi!
Driver:	'aywa, **rayHeen fein?**
Bill:	**MaSr iggideeda.**
Driver:	**fein fi maSr iggideeda?**
Bill:	huteil sheratun.
Driver:	da bεeed, aakhud εashara gneih.
Bill:	**la' εashara kteer.**
Driver:	Tayyib tamanaya.
Catherine:	**tamanya kwayyis.** shukran.
Driver:	itfaDDalu. 'irkabu.

Words and phrases from the dialogue

rayHeen fein?	where are you going?
maSr iggiddeeda	Heliopolis
fein fi maSr iggideeda?	where in Heliopolis?
la' εashara-kteer	no, ten (pounds) is too much
tamanya·kwayyis	eight (pounds) is all right
'irkabu	get in (car)

Useful words and phrases

maHaTTit (maw'af) il'utubees	bus stop
maHaTTit il'aTr	the railway station
'ilmitru	the metro (tram)
mitru-l 'anfaaq	the underground train
'il'utubees da biyrooH . . ?	does this bus go to . . ?
'issouk ('issou')	the market place
'ilkurneish (ikkurneish)	main road by the Nile or the sea
'il'istaad	the stadium

'ilmaTaar	the airport
'utubees εalaTool	direct bus
ilbaa'i*	the change

* **ilbaa'i** literally means the remainder or balance, but it is also used to mean the change from a unit of currency after paying for a purchase or a service.

MaSr This word originally means Egypt, but it is also used in colloquial Egyptian to mean Cairo, so we have **MaSr iggideeda** Heliopolis/New Cairo and **MaSr il'adeema** Old Cairo.

the way it works

Negation

feeh	there is (are)	**mafeesh (maafi)***	there is/are no/not
feeh 'utubees	there is a bus	**mafeesh 'utubees**	there is no bus
feeh shaay	there is tea	**mafeesh 'ahwa**	there is no coffee
feeh bibsi	there is Pepsi	**mafeesh εaSeer**	there is no juice

* **maafi** is non Egyptian

Number

In Arabic, there is singular, dual and plural. The dual is formed by adding **-ein** to masculine words and **-tein** to feminine words ending with **a**. Examples are given in the table below. Note the different pronunciation too.

Singular		Dual		Plural
tazkara (f.)	one ticket	**tazkartein**	two tickets	**tazaakir**
'ouDa (f.)	one room	**'uDtein**	two rooms	**'iwaD**
leila (f.)	one night	**liltein**	two nights	**layaali**
dour (m.)	one floor	**durein**	two floors	**adwaar**
sireer (m.)	one bed	**sirirein**	two beds	**saraayir**
youm (m.)	one day	**yumein**	two days	**ayyaam**

Pronunciation

The prepositions **bi**, **li**, **fi** and **wi** sometimes lose their **i** sound in connected speech when followed or preceeded by the sounds **a**, **i** or **u**.

tighayyaru-*f* baab ilHadeed (fi)	(tighayyaru *fi*)	change at Bab El-Hadid
min hina *lil* haram (li)	(*li* ilharam)	from here to the Pyramids
'ittazkara-*b* kaam (bi)	('ittazkara *bi*)	for how much is the ticket
khamsa-*w* εishreen (wi)	(kham*sa wi* εishreen)	twenty-five

things to do

3.3   Ask the following questions in Arabic:

1   How can I go to the market place?
2   Can we take a taxi from here?
3   Which bus goes to Heliopolis?
4   Where do we change?
5   Where in Giza?

3.4   Clare wants to go to the Andalus Hotel. Translate her conversation into Arabic.

1   Clare: I would like to go to Andalus Hotel.
2   Nadya: You should take a taxi.
3   Laila: Clare can take a bus.
4   Clare: Is there a direct bus?
5   Laila: No, you have to change at Bab ElHadid.
6   Clare: Where is the bus stop?
7   Laila: In front of the bank.
8   Clare: How much is the ticket?
9   Laila: The ticket is twenty piastres.
10 Clare: Very good.

SIGHTSEEING

Some museums and tourist sites are closed on public holidays. It is advisable to check with the tourist information offices or your hotel reception before you decide where to go.

nirooH fein inniharda?/Where shall we go today?

Mr and Mrs Clark have met an Egyptian couple, Mr and Mrs Zaki, at their hotel, and now they ask them about tourist sites in Cairo.

Mrs Clark:	**nirooH fein inniharda?**
Mrs Zaki:	**laazim tirooHu-l matHaf ilmaSri.**
Mr Clark:	**feeh 'eih fil matHaf ilmaSri?**
Mr Zaki:	'ilmatHaf ilmaSri **feeh 'asaar maSriyya 'adeema-kteer.**
Mrs Clark:	**nirooH izzaay** ilmatHaf?
Mr Zaki:	'ilmatHaf fimdaan ittaHreer, mumkin takhdu 'utubees nimra tamanya-w tamaneen
Mr Clark:	**winrooH fein kamaan?**
Mrs Zaki:	**mumkin tizoorul 'azhar wil Hussein wi khaan ilkhaleeli**
Mrs Clark:	Tayyib shukran. **salaam**
Mrs Zaki:	**maɛassalaama. nishufku bukra.**

Words and phrases from the dialogue

nirooH fein inniharda?	Where shall we go today?
laazim tirooHu-l	you should go to the
matHaf ilmaSri	Egyptian museum
feeh 'eih fil . . . ?	What is there in the . . . ?
feeh 'asaar maSriyya 'adeema-kteer	There are many ancient Egyptian
	antiquities (in it).
fimdaan ittaHreer	in the Liberation square.
nirooH izzaay . . . ?	How do we get to . . . ?
winrooH fein kamaan?	Where else can we go?
mumkin tizooru-l 'azhar	You can visit the El-Azhar
wil Husein wi	and El-Hussein and
khaan ilkhaleeli	Khan El-khalili
salaam	cheers, goodbye (short for the Arabic
	greeting **salaamu εaleikum**)
maεassalaama	Goodbye
nishufku bukra	See you tomorrow

Useful words and phrases

Times of the day

The following table shows phrases used to express different times of the day.

Date	Morning	Afternoon	Evening/Night
Today	**inniharda-S SubH**	**baεd iDDuhr**	**billeil**
Yesterday	**imbaariH issubH**	**baεd iDDuhr**	**billeil**
Tomorrow	**bukra-S SubH**	**baεd iDDuhr**	**billeil**

Note the loss of the first vowel in **iSSubH** with **innharda** and **bukra** because of the final vowel in these two words.

Old and new

'adeem (m.)/'adeema (f.)	old, ancient
gideed (m.)/gideeda (f.)	new, modern
εarabiyya 'adeema	old car
gaamiε 'adeem	old mosque
'aasaar 'adeema	ancient antiquities
maSr iggideeda	Heliopolis (the new Cairo)
maSr il'adeema	Old Cairo (the old Cairo)

Big and small

kibeer (m.)/kibeera (f.)	big, large
Sughayyar (m.)/Sughayyara (f.)	small
dukkaan kibeer	big shop
εarabiyya kbeera	big car
gaamiε Sughaayar	small mosque
kineesa-Sghayyra	small church

the way it works

kamaan

kamaan has many meanings depending on the context. It can mean 'also', 'too', 'else', 'another'.

haat waaHid shaay kamaan	bring another tea
wana kamaan	and me too
nirooH fein kamaan?	where else can we go?

nishufku/Goodbye

nishoof means 'we see'. When a personal pronoun is added to it as in **nishufku**, meaning 'we see you', it is used like its English equivalent 'see you' meaning 'goodbye'. Other pronouns can be added as shown below. The words **ashoof** and **nishoof** are used without the pronouns **'ana** (I) or **'iHna** (we).

I	We	Meaning
ashoofak	**nishoofak**	see you (m.)
ashoofik	**nishoofik**	see you (f.)
ashufku	**nishufku**	see you (pl.)

things to do

3.5   You are out sight-seeing in Cairo, say the following in Arabic:

1   I would like to go to El-Azhar.
2   El-Azhar is an old mosque.
3   Khan El-khalili is a big market.
4   What can I see in the museum?
5   How can we go to Khan El-khalili?
6   I would like to see a new mosque.
7   This shop is very small.

SHOPPING FOR FOOD, CLOTHES AND SOUVENIRS

You will find that shops in the Arab countries are usually open from 9.00 a.m. to 9.00 p.m., with a two- or three-hour break in the afternoon. Shops are not closed on both weekend days (Thursday and Friday) but most are closed for part of the weekend. There are specialised small shops, but there are also department stores in big towns which sell a wide variety of goods including clothes (**malaabis** ملابس) and gifts (**hadaaya** هدايا). Many of these stores accept the major credit cards. Be prepared for a different system of paying, however. In bigger shops and supermarkets, after you choose your goods, you are given a bill which you pay at the cash desk (**ilkhazeena**) then you collect your goods from an adjacent counter (**il'istilam**).

shira-l fawaakih/Buying fruit

Bill:	**bikaam keelu-t teen?**
Shopkeeper:	bi talaata gneih.
Bill:	**wi keelu-l εinab?**
Shopkeeper:	bikhamsa gneih.
Bill:	**'iddeeni keelu** teen witnein εinab min faDlak.
Shopkeeper:	HaaDir yafandim.
Bill:	**'ilHisaab kaam** min faDlak?
Shopkeeper:	Hidaashar gineih.
Bill:	'itfaDDal khamasTaashar gineih wi haat ilbaa'i.
Shopkeeper:	ilbaa'i 'arbaεa gneih. 'itfaDDal.

Words and phrases from the dialogue

bikaam keelu-t teen?	how much is a kilo of figs?
wi keelu-l εinab?	and (how much is) a kilo of grapes?
'iddeeni keelu	give me a kilo of
'ilHisaab kaam?	how much is the bill (the lot)?

ilmalaabis wit-tuHaf/Clothes and souvenirs

Catherine:	**εayza jakitta gild** min faDlak.
Shopkeeper:	**ma'aas kaam?**
Catherine:	**ma'aas Sughayyar.**
Shopkeeper:	**feeh bunni-w beij.**
Catherine:	'iddeeni waHda bunni.
Shopkeeper:	'itfaDDali. bi miyya warbiεeen gineih.
Catherine:	la' **di ghalya kida. wishshanTa di-b kaam?**
Shopkeeper:	bitalateen gineih.
Catherine:	Tayyib 'aakhud iljakitta-l bunni wishshanTa-b miyya-w khamseen gineih.
Shopkeeper:	miyya-w sitteen kwayyis.
Catherine:	Tayyib, itfaDDal, 'aadi miyya-w sitteen.
Shopkeeper:	shukran, maεassalama.

Words and phrases from the dialogue

jakitta gild	leather jacket
ma'aas kaam?	what size?
ma'aas Sughayyar	small size
feeh bunni-w beij.	there is brown and beige.
di ghalya kida	this is expensive at this price.
wishshanTa di-b kaam?	and how much is this handbag?

shira-l kuroot/Buying cards

Mrs Clark:	**mumkin ashoof ilkuroot** min faDlik?
Assistant:	itfaDDali. εayza kaam kart?
Mrs Clark:	**la' mish doul, 'ana εayza kart bustaal**.
Assistant:	feeh kart bustaal. HaaDir.

Mrs Clark:	bikaam ilkart?
Assistant:	ilkart bi khamasTaashar 'irsh.
Mrs Clark:	Tayyib, **'iddeeni khamas kuroot**.
Assistant:	khamsa-w sabɛeen 'irsh, min faDlik.
Mrs Clark:	'itfaDDali gineih wi haati-l baa'i.
Assistant:	ilbaa'i khamsa-w ɛishreen 'irsh. 'itfaDDali.
Mrs Clark:	shukran.
Assistant:	ilɛafw, maɛassalaama.

Words and phrases from the dialogue

mumkin ashoof ilkuroot?	can I see the cards?
ɛayza kaam kart?	how many cards do you want?
la' mish doul	no, not these ones
kart bustaal	post cards
'iddeeni khamas kuroot	give me five cards

Bargaining

di ghalya (f.)/**da ghaali** (m.)	this is expensive
di-rkheeSa (f.)/**da-rkheeS** (m.)	this is cheap
feeh 'arkhaS min kida?	is there anything cheaper than that?
kwayyis kida.	that is all right.

Colours

(m.)	(f.)		(m.)	(f.)	
abyaD	**beiDa**	white	**akhDar**	**khaDra**	green
iswid	**souda**	black	**azra'**	**zar'a**	blue
aHmar	**Hamra**	red	**bunni**	**bunni**	brown
aSfar	**Safra**	yellow	**beij**	**beij**	beige

the way it works

Masculine and feminine words

Feminine words usually end with the sound **a** as in **jakitta**, **gazma**, **vaaza**, **ɛilba**. When using colour words the feminine form should be used to describe feminine objects.

Examples

Feminine			Masculine		
jakitta	souda	black jacket	gamal	aHmar	red camel
vaaza	KhaDra	green vase	bantaloun	bunni	brown trousers
gazma	beiDa	white shoes	'ameeS	'abyaD	white shirt
bilouza	Hamra	red blouse	Taba'	'aHmar	red plate

When making the objects definite, the colour words also become definite e.g. **iljakitta-l bunni (il bunni), il'ameeS il'abyaD**.

Plurals

Many feminine words ending in **a**, have **aat** in the plural e.g. **jakitta→jakittaat** and **vaaza→vazaat**. However, as many other different patterns are used to make plurals in Arabic, you will have to learn most plurals as you go along.

Examples

Singular	Plural	Singular	Plural
kart	kuroot	ɛilba	ɛilab
'irsh	'uroosh	shanTa	shunaT
tazkara	tazaakir	gaamiɛ	gawaamiɛ
maTɛam	maTaaɛim	kineesa	kanaayis
gamal	gimaal	Taba'	'aTbaa'
timsaal	tamaseel	Saniyya	Sawaani
galabiyya	galaleeb	maktaba	maktabaat
banTaloun	banTalunaat	'ameeS	'umSaan
gazma	gizam	'ouDa	'iwaD
'utubees	'utubisaat	hidiyya	hadaaya

Cardinal numbers revisited

There are two forms of cardinal numbers from 3 to 10. One form is used for telling the time, ordering food or drinks and talking about money. The counted objects (see p. 15) are usually expressed in the singular with this form.

The other form is used for counting everything else, and it is usually followed by the plural form of the object counted as shown below.

talat tazaakir	three tickets	**sabaɛ gimaal**	seven camels
arbaɛ ɛilab	four boxes	**taman Sawaani**	eight trays
khamas kuroot	five cards	**tisaɛ 'iwaD**	nine rooms
sitt biluzaat	six blouses	**ɛashar 'aTbaa'**	ten plates

things to do

4.1 Ask about the prices of the following:
1. A kilo of mangoes.
2. A kilo of strawberries.
3. The green jacket.
4. The beige shirt.
5. This statue.

4.2 Say the following to shopkeepers:
1. No, this is expensive (blouse).
2. O.K., give me six cards.
3. I'll take the red camel.
4. I'll take three galabiyyas.
5. Here's five pounds and give me the change.

POSTING LETTERS AND MAKING TELEPHONE CALLS

Post offices in Arab countries are open every day except for Fridays and holidays. Opening hours differ from one country to another. In Egypt, they are generally open from 8 a.m. to 2 p.m. Some branches in larger cities may stay open as late as 8 p.m. Delivery times for international mail can be improved if you write the name of the destination country in Arabic.

fi maktab ilbareed/At the post office

Bill:	**ɛaayiz Tawaabiɛ likhamas gawabaat** min faDlak.
Clerk:	**ilgawabaat rayHa fein?**
Bill:	'ingiltira.
Clerk:	**bareed gawwi walla ɛaadi?**
Bill:	bareed gawwi min faDlak.
Clerk:	talaata gneih. **iTTaabiɛ bi sitteen 'irsh.**
Bill:	**wi ɛaayiz 'abɛat ilgawaab da musaggal.**
Clerk:	ilmusaggal lingiltira miyya-w sitteen 'irsh. **Haaga tanya?**
Bill:	la' shukran **khalaaS.**
Clerk:	**ilmagmooɛ 'arbaɛa gneih** wi sitteen 'irsh.
Bill:	itfaDDal. (handing the money)
Clerk:	shukran. **wi da waSl ittasgeel.**

Words and phrases from the dialogue

ɛaayiz Tawaabiɛ	can I have stamps
likhamas gawabaat	for five letters
ilgawabaat rayHa fein?	where are the letters going?
bareed gawwi walla ɛaadi?	by air mail or surface mail?
'iTTaabiɛ bi sitteen 'irsh	sixty piastres each (stamp)
wi ɛaayiz 'abɛat	and I would like to send
ilgawaab da musaggal	this letter by recorded delivery
Haaga tanya?	anything else?
khalaaS	that's it
'ilmagmuuɛ 'arbaɛa gneih	the total is four pounds
wi da waSl ittasgeel	and this is the receipt for the recorded delivery

Useful words and phrases

bareed	post
Taabiɛ bareed	postage stamp
Sanduu' ilbareed	posting box
bareed gawwi	air mail
biTTayyara	by air mail (by plane)
ɛaayiz abɛat	I would like to send (post)
ilgawaab da biTTayyaara	this letter by air
ilgawaab da musaggal	this letter by recorded delivery
ilkart da 'ingiltira	this card to England
ɛaayiz asaggil ilgawaab da (or) ɛaayiz abɛat ilgawaab da musaggal	I would like to send this letter by recorded delivery
walla/aw	or

Singular and plural

Singular		Plural	
gawaab	letter	gawabaat	letters
ilgawaab	the letter	ilgawabaat	the letters
kart	card	kuroot	cards
'ilkart	the card	ilkuroot	the cards
Tard	parcel	Turood	parcels
iTTard	the parcel	iTTurood	the parcels
Taabiɛ	stamp	Tawaabiɛ	stamps
'iTTaabiɛ	the stamp	iTTawaabiɛ	the stamps

Making a phone call

You can make local and international telephone calls at your hotel or at public telephone offices. Local calls can also be made from public telephones in the streets, in some countries, or from most shops, which charge a reasonable fee. It is more convenient to use the hotel telephones, but it is cheaper to use the telephone office, particularly for international calls. In hotels you ask the operator to connect you to local or international numbers. In the public telephone office you book the call with an assistant, wait until your number is obtained then the assistant calls you to take the call from booth number such and such. After you finish your call, you pay the fees and get a receipt.

fi-s sintiraal/At the telephone office

Catherine:	ɛayza mukalma manshistar min faDlak.
Clerk:	HaaDir. nimra kaam fi manshistar?
Catherine:	innimra di. (shows him the number written)
Clerk:	kaam di'ee'a?
Catherine:	sitt da'aayi' min faDlak. bikaam?
Clerk:	arbaɛa-w ɛishreen gineih.
Catherine:	Tayyib shukran.
Clerk:	itfaDDali, kabeena nimra sabɛa.

Words and phrases from the dialogue

ɛayza mukalma manshistar	I would like to call Manchester
nimra kaam	what is the number?
kaam di'ee'a?	how many minutes?
sitt da'aayi'	six minutes
kabeena nimra sabɛa	cabin (booth) No. 7

Useful words and phrases

ɛaayiz/ɛayza (f.) akallim landan	I would like to make a call to London
mumkin akallim London?	can (may) I make a call to London?
mumkin aɛmil tilifoun?	can I make a call?
mumkin akkallim fittilifoun?	can I use the phone?
ilmukalma khamseen 'irsh	50 piastres a call
'aloo/'alu	hello (on the phone)
'aywa, meen?	yes, who is it? (calling)

the way it works

ɛaadi means 'ordinary'. When talking about post, it means surface mail.
khalaaS means 'finished'. It is used in conversation to mean 'that's it', 'that's all', 'no more', 'it's finished', or 'already'.

things to do

4.3 Say the following in Arabic:

1 I would like to send these cards to Birmingham.
2 Can I send this letter, recorded delivery, please?
3 Can I send these parcels to Paris, please?
4 I would like a stamp for this card, please.
5 I would like to send these letters by air mail.
6 Where is the recording receipt?
7 How much is a stamp for Britain by air mail?
8 Can I use the telephone?
9 Can I call Alexandria?
10 I would like to call Manchester, please.

LONG-DISTANCE TRAVEL

There are intercity air and bus services in all the Arab countries, but railway services are only available in some. Trains have three classes, with a 'superluxe' class on certain routes, which provides air conditioned carriages and sleeping compartments, and buffet or restaurant services. It is advisable to travel at least first class on trains, especially as the fares are reasonable. Third class is very basic (wooden seats); and the locals would also be surprised to see you among them in second class. Air conditioned buses also run on certain bus routes.

You should enquire about the facilities available on the route you are using before booking train or bus tickets and be sure to reserve seats in advance, particularly for longer journeys.

Look for the following signs:

Ticket office	shibbaak ittazaakir	شباك التذاكر
Platform number	raSeef raqam	رصيف رقم...
Carriage number	ɛaraba raqam	عربة رقم...
Restaurant carriage	ɛarabiyyit il'akl	عربة الأكل
Sleeping carriage	ɛarabiyyit innoum	عربة النوم

issafar bil'aTr/Travelling by train

It would be useful to refer to pp. 26–28 for talking about time in this unit.

Bill: **tazkara skindiriyya** min faDlak.
Clerk: **daraga 'oola walla tanya?**
Bill: **daraga 'oola mukayyafa.**
Clerk: **raayiH gayy walla raayiH bass?**
Bill: raayiH gayy.
Clerk: daraga 'oola raayiH gayy, bi ɛashara gneih.
Bill: itfaDDal. **il'aTr issaaɛa kaam?**
Clerk: feeh 'aTr issaaɛa tamanya-w nuSS.
Bill: **raSeef nimra kaam?**
Clerk: **raSeef nimra talaata.**
Bill: feeh ɛarabiyyit 'akl?
Clerk: 'aywa feeh. **wi feeh bufeih kamaan.**

Words and phrases from the dialogue

tazkara skindiriyya	a ticket to Alexandria
daraga 'oola	1st class
walla tanya?	or 2nd class?
daraga 'oola mukayyafa	1st class air-conditioned
raayiH gayy	return
walla raayiH bass?	or one way only?
il'aTr issaaɛa kaam?	what time is the train?
feeh 'aTr	there is a train
issaaɛa tamanya-w nuSS.	at 8.30.
raSeef nimra kaam?	what platform number?
raSeef nimra talaata	platform No. 3
feeh ɛarabiyyit 'akl?	is there a restaurant carriage?
wi feeh bufeih kamaan.	and there is a buffet as well.

Useful words and phrases

'aTr iskindiriyya (lukSur, etc)	the train to Alexandria (Luxor, etc)
ɛaayiz aHgiz makaan	I would like to book a seat
iddeeni tazkara	give me a ticket
daraga 'oola (tanya)	1st (2nd) class
siyaHiyya	tourist class (on planes)
feeh makaan ('amaakin)	there is a seat (are seats)
mafeesh 'amaakin fi	there are no seats on
'aTr 'issaaɛa khamsa	the 5 o'clock train
Tayyaarit issaaɛa khamsa	the 5 o'clock plane

feeh makaan waaHid bass.	there is only one seat
raayiH/zahaab	one way
raayiH gayy/zahaab wi ɛawda	return
misaafir (misafreen) *imta?*	*when* are you travelling?
raagiɛ (ragɛeen) *imta?*	*when* are you coming back?
misaafir biTTayyara	travelling by plane (air)
misaafir bil'aTr	travelling by train
fi ɛarabiyyit innoum	in the sleeping carriage
diwaan bisrirein	compartment with two berths
riHla raqam	flight number
iTTayyaara t'oom issaaɛa kaam?	what times does the plane take off?
iTTayyara tiwSal issaaɛa kaam?	what time does the plane arrive?
iTTayyaara *t'oom min* . . . issaaɛa	the plane *takes off* from . . . at . . . o'clock
iTTayyaara *tiwSal* . . . issaaɛa	the plane *arrives at* . . . at . . . o'clock
il'aTr-i y'oom issaaɛa kaam?	what time does the train leave?
il'aTr yiwSal issaaɛa kaam?	what time does the train arrive?

things to do

5.1 You are booking seats for yourself and friends on a train from Cairo to Luxor. Say the following to the ticket officer, in Arabic. You and the ticket officer are both male. (Refer to pp. 26–28 and p. 80 when talking about time.)

1 What time is the train to Luxor?
2 We are travelling on Friday morning.
3 I would like to book four seats, please.
4 First class air-conditioned.
5 We are going by train and coming back by plane.
6 Can I book a compartment with two berths?
7 How much is the ticket?
8 Is there a restaurant carriage?
9 What time does the train leave?
10 And what time does it arrive?

5.2 You are booking a plane seat for yourself from Amman to Jeddah. Say the following in Arabic. You and the ticket officer are both female.

1 I would like to book a seat to Jeddah.
2 I am travelling Friday afternoon.
3 How much is a return ticket?
4 Tourist class.
5 What time does the plane take off?
6 What time does the plane arrive in Jeddah?

SPORT AND LEISURE

Most big hotels have sports facilities, particularly for swimming, tennis, squash and table tennis. There are also sporting clubs which are similar to sports centres in Britain, except that, in some countries, you cannot be admitted unless you are accompanied by a club member. In the evening various kinds of shows are presented in the hotels, theatres, cinemas, music halls and night clubs.

il 'alɛaab irriyaaDiyya/Sports activities

Bill and Catherine make enquiries at the hotel reception about the sports facilities available.

Bill: **'iHna ɛayzeen nilɛab tinis niɛmil 'eih?**
Receptionist: **tiHgizu malɛab. ɛayzeen tilɛabu 'add 'eih?**
Bill: **saaɛa-kfaaya. wi baɛdein niɛoom shiwayya.**
Receptionist: issaaɛ-b khamsa-gneih. ɛanduku maDaarib?
Bill: **la' maɛandinaash maDaarib hina.**
Receptionist: **mumkin ti'aggaru maDaarib min il huteil.**
Bill: Tayyib ni'aggar maDrabein.
Receptionist: laaz'im tiHgizu-l malɛab **bisurɛa.**

Catherine:	wi **Hammaam issibaaHa ɛaayiz Hagz?**
Receptionist:	la'. Hammaam issibaaHa ɛaayiz **rasm-idkhool**.
Catherine:	wi rasm iddukhool kaam?
Receptionist:	gineih **likull waaHid**.
Bill:	Tayyib shukran.
Receptionist:	ma'assalaama.

Words and phrases from the dialogue

'iHna ɛayzeen nilɛab tinis	we would like to play tennis
niɛmil 'eih?	what shall we do?
tiHgizu malɛab	(you) book a court.
ɛayzeen tilɛabu 'add 'eih?	how long do you want to play?
saaɛa kfaaya	an hour is enough.
niɛoom shiwayya	(we) swim for a bit.
ɛanduku maDaarib	do you have rackets?
maɛandinaash maDaarib	we have no rackets.
mumkin ti'aggaru maDaarib	you can hire rackets.
bisurɛa	quickly.
Hammaam issibaaHa	the swimming pool
ɛaayiz hagz?	does it need booking?
rasm-idkhool	entrance fee
likull waaHid	each

Useful words and phrases

Hammaam sibaaHa	swimming pool
malɛab tinis/iskwaash	tennis/squash court
tarabeizit bing bong	table tennis table
maDrab tinis/iskwaash	tennis/squash racket
kourit tinis/iskwaash	tennis/squash ball
ilmaDaarib *maggaanan*	the rackets *are free*
Hammaam issibaaHa *maggaanan*	the swimming pool *is free*
nilɛab sawa (maɛa baɛD)	let's play together
fi-n naadi	in the club

nirooH fein?/Where to go?

Mr and Mrs Clark ask their hotel manager for advice on spending the evening out in Luxor.

Mr Clark:	**nirooH fein i'llilaadi?**
Manager:	feeh **birnaamig iSSouT wiDDou'** fi maɛbad ilkarnaK.
Mrs Clark:	wifeeh 'eih kamaan?
Manager:	feeh **sahra maSriyya** hina fil huteil.
Mr Clark:	issahra-l maSriyya **feeha 'eih?**
Manager:	feeha **museeqa maSriyya** wi **ra'S shaɛbi** wi **'aghaani** shaɛbiyya.

Mr Clark:	wifeeh 'eih kamaan?
Manager:	wifeeh **sahra 'urubbiyya** fi huteil ramsees.
Mrs Clark:	iSSouT wiDDou' issaaɛa kaam?
Manager:	**ilbirnaamig yibda'** issaaɛa sabɛa, **wi yintihi-s saaɛa** ɛashara.
Mrs Clark:	Tayyib **nirooH iSSout** wiDDou' **inniharda, winiHDar** issahra-l maSriyya **bukra**.
Manager:	**tisharrafu** yafandim.

Words and phrases from the dialogue

nirooH fein illilaadi?	where shall we go this evening?
birnaamig iSSout wiDDou'	the son et lumière programme
fi maɛbad ilkarnak	in Karnak temple
wifeeh 'eih kamaan?	and what else is there?
sahra maSriyya ('urubbiyya)	Egyptian (European) evening entertainment
feeha 'eih?	what is in it?
museeqa maSriyya	Egyptian music
ra'S shaɛbi	folk dances
'aghaani shaɛbiyya	folk songs
ilbirnaamig yibda'	the programme starts
wi yintihi-s saaɛa	and ends at . . . o'clock
nirooH . . . inniharda	we go to . . . today
winiHDar . . . bukra	and attend . . . tomorrow
tisharrafu	it is an honour to us

Useful words and phrases

sinama	cinema
masraH	theatre
film	film
masraHiya	play
'ana harooH ilmasraH	I am going to the theatre
'ana harooH issinama	I am going to the cinema
'ana harooH il'ahwa	I am going to the café
'ana harooH disco	I am going to a disco
'ana hatfarrag ɛala-t tilifizioun	I am going to watch television
'ana hatfarrag ɛala-l vidyu	I am going to watch the video
'ana hatfarrag ɛala-k koura	I am going to watch the football
'ahwa ɛala-n neel/-lbaHr	a café by the Nile/sea
tiHibb-i-trooH fein?	where would you like to go?

the way it works

Sports

il'alɛaab irriyaaDiyya is a term used in Arabic when talking about all kinds of sports activities whether they are games or sports. The singular of **'alɛaab** is **liɛba**.

malɛab is used in Arabic to mean pitch, field or court. The plural is **malaaɛib**.

malɛab/malaaɛib tinis	tennis court/s
malɛab/ malaaɛib koura	football pitch/es
malɛab/malaaɛib huki	hockey pitch/es
malɛab/malaaɛib iskwash	squash court/s
malɛab/malaaɛib vuli	volleyball court/s

Some

shiwayya means 'a bit', 'a little' or 'some'. When it is followed by a noun it becomes **shiwayyit**.

Examples

shiwayyit mayya	some water
shiwayyit teen	some figs
ilɛab shiwayya	play for a bit

Verbs in the future

ha at the beginning of the verb makes it future.

Examples

'ana *ha*tfarrag	I am going to (shall) watch
'iHna *ha*nitfarrag	we are going to (shall) watch
huwwa *ha*yitfarrag	he is going to (will) watch

55

In some cases the first vowel of the verb is dropped.

'ana harooh (arooH)	I shall go
iHna hanrooh (nirooH)	we shall go
huwwa hayrooH (yirooH)	he will go

things to do

5.3 Tom wants to play squash. Translate the conversation he has into Arabic.

1	Tom:	Can I book a squash court?
2	Attendant:	For how long?
3	Tom:	One hour.
4	Attendant:	Do you want rackets?
5	Tom:	No, we have rackets.
6	Attendant:	Five pounds please.
7	Tom:	When can we play?
8	Attendant:	Half past four.
9	Tom:	Is there a shower here?
10	Attendant:	Yes, there are three.
11	Tom:	Where are they?
12	Attendant:	At the end of this corridor, on the left.

5.4 Nabeel asks Peter where he would like to spend the evening. Translate Peter's part into Arabic.

	Nabeel:	Where would you like to go tonight?
1	Peter:	What's available?
	Nabeel:	There is a nice programme in the club.
2	Peter:	What else is there?
	Nabeel:	There is also evening entertainment in the hotel.
3	Peter:	What does the hotel evening include?
	Nabeel:	The hotel evening entertainment is a programme of Egyptian music and songs?
4	Peter:	And what does the club evening include?
	Nabeel:	The club programme is European music and singing.
5	Peter:	All right. We'll go to the club tonight.

HEALTH PROBLEMS

There are both public and private health services in the Arab countries. Public services are available in government hospitals and medical centres. Private services are available in private hospitals and surgeries. If you are too ill to move, you can ask for a doctor to come and see you, or for an ambulance to take you to the nearest hospital or medical centre. In case of emergency you can go, or be taken, to the casualty department in any hospital, public or private.

Doctors speak English, but your knowledge of Arabic would be useful for talking to hotel staff, ambulance men, paramedics or members of the public in case of emergency. It is advisable to take medical insurance before you travel so that you can claim any expenses.

taɛbaan shiwayya/Feeling ill

Mr Clark does not feel well when he gets up in the morning. Mrs Clark rings the hotel reception to ask their advice.

Mrs Clark:	SabaaH ilkheir, 'ana misiz klaark, 'ouDa nimra arbaɛTaashar.
Reception:	SabaaH ilkheir yamadaam. 'ayyi khidma?
Mrs Clark:	'ana zougi **taɛbaan shiwayya. niɛmil 'eih?**
Reception:	**huwwa ɛandu 'eih** yamadaam?
Mrs Clark:	**ɛandu Sudaaɛ w-iltihaab fi zouru**
Reception:	**tiHibbi niTlublu duktour?**
Mrs Clark:	'aywa min faDlik.
Reception:	Tayyib, **haniTlub duktour Haalan.**
Mrs Clark:	shukran.
Reception:	ilɛafw.

Words and phrases in the dialogue

taɛbaan shiwayya	is not very well
niɛmil 'eih?	what shall we do?
huwwa ɛandu 'eih?	what is wrong with him?/what does he suffer from?
ɛandu Sudaaɛ	he has a headache
w-iltihaab fi zouru	and a sore throat
tiHibbi niTlublu duktour?	would you like us to call a doctor for him?
haniTlub duktour Haalan	we shall call a doctor immediately

fil ɛiyaada/In the surgery

Bill goes to see a doctor because he has a stomach-ache.

Doctor:	ɛandak éih ya mistar teilar?
Bill:	**ɛandi maghaS wi 'is-haal.**
Doctor:	**min 'imta?**
Bill:	**min imbaariH billeil.**
Doctor:	Tayyib **'aakhud ilHaraara.**

After taking Bill's temperature and examining him, the doctor gives him a prescription.

Doctor:	**mafeesh Haraara. di Haaga baseeTa. khud iddawa da wistareeH raaHa kamla.**
Bill:	'aakhud iddawa **kaam marra?**
Doctor:	**talat marraat fil youm** baɛd il'akl.
Bill:	**waakul 'eih?**
Doctor:	**Kul tust wishrab Hagaat sa'ɛa bass.**
Bill:	shukran ya duktour salaamu ɛaleiku.
Doctor:	ilɛafw maɛassalaama.

Words and phrases from the dialogue

ɛandi maghaS wi 'is-haal	I have stomach-ache and diarrhoea
min 'imta?	Since when?
min imbaariH billeil	Since last night
'aakhud ilHaraara	Let me take the temperature
mafeesh Haraara	There is no temperature
di Haaga baseeTa	This is not serious
khud iddawa da	Take this medicine
wistareeH raaHa kamla	and have complete rest
kaam marra?	how often?
talat marraat fil youm	Three times a day
waakul 'eih?	And what shall I eat?
kul tust	eat toast
wishrab Hagaat sa'ɛa	and have cold drinks
bass	only

Describing your ailments

There are two different ways of talking about ailments
1 εandi + symptom = I have + symptom
2 (part of the body) bi yiwgaεni (m.)/bi tiwgaεni (f.)

Examples

1 εandi Sudaaε   I have a headache
   εandi imsaak   I have constipation
   εandi iltihaab fi zouri   I have a sore throat

2 kitfi-b yiwgaεni (m.)   I have pain in my shoulder
   diraaεi-b yiwgaεni (m.)   I have pain in my arm
   rigli-b tiwgaεni (f.)   I have pain in my leg
   'ieedi-b tiwgaεni (f.)   I have pain in my hand
   (Note the change of **bi** into -**b**.)

Injuries

pronoun	twisted	cut	broke
I/You	laweit	garaHt	kasart
He	lawa	garaH	kasar
She	lawit	garaHit	kasarit

Examples

'ana laweit diraaεi	I twisted my arm
Nabeel kasar diraaεu	Nabeel broke his arm
Fayza garaHit 'idha	Fayza cut her hand

Other injuries

'araSni dabboor	*I have been stung* by a wasp
'araSitni naHla	*I have been stung* by a bee

Things you have to tell the doctor

'ana εandi sukkar	I am diabetic
'ana εandi rabw	I am asthmatic
'ana εandi-l 'alb (εandi il'alb)	I have heart trouble
'ana εandi Hasasiya lil binsileen	I am allergic to penicillin
'ana Haamil	I am pregnant

Asking for help

εaayiz duktour (m.)	I need a doctor
εayza duktour (f.)	I need a doctor
εaayiz il'isεaaf (m.)	I need the ambulance
εayza-l 'isεaaf (f.)	I need the ambulance
εaayiz arooH ilmustashfa (m.)	I want to go to the hospital.

Key words in Arabic

Ambulance	il'isεaaf	الاسعاف	Surgery	εiyaada	عيادة
Hospital	mustashfa	مستشفى	Doctor	duktour	دكتور

the way it works

'istareeH means have a rest, so **istareeH raaHa kamla** means have a complete rest. But in the phrase **itfaDDal istareeH** it means take a seat or have a seat.

Negation

mish, mafeesh, maɛandeesh

mish	not
mish ɛaarif	I don't know
mish raayiH	I am not going

mafeesh	there is no (not)
mafeesh Haraara	there is no temperature
mafeesh ɛaSeer	there is no juice

maɛandeesh	I have no (not)
maɛandeesh Haraara	I have not got a temperature

Orders and requests

The doctor might tell you to do the following:

person	take	eat	drink
singular (m.)	**khud**	**kul**	**ishrab**
singular (f.)	**khudi**	**kuli**	**ishrabi**
plural (m. + f.)	**khudu**	**kulu**	**ishrabu**

things to do

6.1 Tell the doctor what each member of the group is suffering from.

1 Tom suffers from toothache.
2 Laura has a cold.
3 Josephine has a sore throat.
4 Helen has a sore eye.
5 Henry has heartburn.

6.2 Translate the following questions into English and give the answers in Arabic.

1	ɛandak bard?	No, I haven't
2	ɛandik Haraara?	Yes, I have
3	ɛankak Hasasiya lilbinsileen?	No, I haven't
4	min 'imta?	Since this morning
5	feeh Sudaaɛ?	No, there isn't

youm issabt/Saturday

fil agzakhaana/At the pharmacy

Catherine:	mumkin **Haaga lil HumooDa**, min faDlak?
Chemist:	'aywa feeh **dawa shurb** mumtaaz.
Catherine:	**'aakhud 'add'eih?**
Chemist:	khudi **maɛla'a-kbeera marritein fil youm. marra**-S SubH, **wi marra** billeil.
Catherine:	baɛd il'akl walla 'abl il'akl?
Chemist:	baɛd il'akl.
Catherine:	shukran. 'ilHisaab kaam?
Chemist:	miyya-w khamseen 'irsh, bass.
Catherine:	'itfaDDal.
Chemist:	shukran. maɛassalaama.

Words and phrases from the dialogue

Haaga lil HumooDa	something for heartburn
dawa shurb	liquid medicine to take orally
'aakhud 'add'eih?	how much shall I take?
maɛla'a-kbeera	one tablespoonful
marritein fil youm	twice a day
marra . . . wi marra	once . . . and once . . .

Useful words and phrases

dawa 'a'raaS	medicine in tablet form (tablets)
dawa saayil (shurb)	medicine in liquid form (liquid)
dawa Hu'an	medicine to be taken by injection
'urS ('a'raaS)	tablet (tablets)
mumkin Haaga (dawa) li?	can I have something/medicine for?
ɛaayiz *Haaga (dawa) li	I want something/medicine for
ɛaayiz aSrif iddawa da	I want this medicine made up
ɛaayiz aSrif irrushitta di	I want this prescription made up
'add 'eih?	how much?
kaam marra?	how many times?
maɛla'a-kbeera	tablespoonful
maɛla'a-Sghayyara	teaspoonful

* Note: Use **ɛaayiz** if a man, **ɛayza** if a woman.

61

the way it works

Big and small

Kibeera   big   **sughayyara**   small
When talking about dosage in medicine **maɛla'a-kbeera** means 'tablespoonful' and **maɛla'a-Sghayyara** means 'teaspoonful'. **Kbeera** and **Sghayyaara** lost their first vowels because of the last **a** in **maɛla'a**.

How many?

kaam?   How many?
kaam is always followed by the singular when asking about the number of anything.

Examples

kaam marra?	how many times?
kaam keelu?	how many kilos?
kaam gineih?	how many pounds?

The answer to **kaam marra?** can be as follows

marra waHda	once
marritein	twice
talat marraat	times (up to 10)
Hidaashar marra	eleven times (from 11 upwards)

things to do

6.3   Ask in Arabic for the following things at the pharmacy:

1   something for a headache
2   to have a prescription made up
3   shaving cream and toothpaste
4   cotton wool, Dettol and elastoplast
5   something for diarrhoea and a disinfectant
6   how many times you should take the medicine
7   how much of the medicine you should take
8   a toothbrush
9   eau de Cologne and talcum powder
10   shaving brush and razor blades

EATING OUT

Lunch (**'ilghada**) is the main meal for townspeople in Egypt and all other Arab countries. A formal lunch is a four course meal, whether it is served at a restaurant, in a hotel or in a private house. Lunch (**'ilghada**) is served between 1.00 and 4.00 in the afternoon. The evening meal (**'ilεasha**) is either a big meal, like lunch, or a light meal. Light meals, if not taken at home, are served in restaurants and cafés.

A formal meal includes the following:

shurba 'aw salaTa	soup or salad
ruzz 'aw makarouna	rice or macaroni
laHma-w khuDaar wi salaTa	meat, vegetables and salad
il Hilw	dessert
mashroub (shaay/'ahwa)	drink (tea or coffee)

Although alcoholic drinks are only available in some Arab countries, non-alcoholic beer (**beera**) and wine (**nibeet**) are available in them all. The majority of the Arab people have water (**mayya**) or fizzy drinks with their big meals.

Waiters expect a tip (**ba'sheesh**) even if a service charge is included in the bill. A 10% tip is just right in all kinds of restaurants.

fil maTεam/At the restaurant

Kamaal Salem and his wife arranged to meet Bill and Catherine and give them a meal at a restaurant in Cairo.

Kamaal: massaa' ilkheir. εayzeen **tarabeiza larbaεa** min faDlak.
Waiter: 'ahlan yafandim. **itfaDDalu min hina.**
Kamaal: **mumkin il minyu** min faDlak?
Waiter: **Haalan** yafandim.

Later, after consulting the menu. . .

Waiter: 'aywa yafandim, **Talabatku 'eih**?
Kamaal: ɛayzeen itnein **shurbit ɛats** witnein shurbit **TamaaTim**.
Waiter: ɛeish wi **salaTaat wi-mkhallilaat**?
Kamaal: 'aywa. wi baɛdein ɛayzeen itnein ruzz, witnein makarouna,
          witnein kabaab, witnein kufta-w waaHid bamya-w waaHid
          bisilla.
Waiter: **tiHibbu tishrabu eih maɛa-l 'akl**?
Kamaal: naakhud arbaɛa ɛaSeer tuffaaH, **wi-'zaazit mayya maɛdaniyya**.
Waiter: **wil Hilw**?
Kamaal: 'itnein mihallabiyya-w waaHid baTTeekh wi waaHid ɛinab.
Waiter: tiHibbu 'ahwa walla shaay **baɛd il'akl**?
Kamaal: 'itnein **'ahwa maZbooT**, witnein **shaay biniɛnaaɛ**.
Waiter: HaaDir yafandim. 'ayyi khidma.

Kamaal: **ilHisaab min faDlak**.
Waiter: HaaDir, **sanya waHda. itfaDDal**.
Kamaal: dal Hisaab, **wida ɛashaanak**.
Waiter: shukran maɛassalaama.

Words and phrases from the dialogue

tarabeiza larbaɛa	a table for four
itfaDDalu min hina	This way please
mumkin il minyu?	Can we have the menu?
Haalan	In a minute (literally it means immediately)
Talabatku 'eih?	what would you like to order?
shurbit ɛats/TamaaTim	lentil/tomato soup
salaTaat wi-mkhallilaat	salads and pickles
tiHibbu tishrabu 'eih maɛa-l 'akl?	what would you like to drink with the meal?
'izaazit mayya	a bottle of water
mayya maɛdaniyya	mineral water
wil Hilw?	and what for dessert?
baɛd il'akl?	after the meal?
'ahwa maZbooT	Turkish coffee with little sugar
shaay biniɛnaaɛ	mint tea (with mint)
ilHisaab min faDlak	the bill, please
sanya waHda	one second
wida ɛashaanak	and this is for you

Useful words and phrases

'ana Haagiz tarabeiza	I have booked a table	I (m.)
'ana Hagza tarabeiza	I have booked a table	I (f.)
'iHna Hagzeen tarabeiza	we have booked a table	we (m./f.)
'abl il'akl	before the meal/food	
maɛa-l 'akl	with the meal/food	
baɛd il 'akl	after the meal/food	

The word **Haaga** which means 'thing' is always used when asking for drinks of any kind. Hot or cold is **sukhna** or **sa'ɛa**.

Examples

mumkin Haaga sa'ɛa?	can I have a cold drink?
mumkin nishrab Haaga?	can we have something to drink?

Another way of asking for a drink is mentioning it by name.

Examples

mumkin nishrab shaay?	can we have tea?
'ahwa min faDlak	coffee please

Asking about food and drinks available

ɛanduku shurbit 'eih?	what soup have you got?
ɛanduku (feeh) khuDaar 'eih?	what vegetables have you got?
ɛanduku'eih saa'iɛ?	what cold drinks have you got?
ɛanduku ɛaSeer 'eih?	what juices have you got?
ɛanduku Hilw 'eih?	what dessert have you got?
ɛanduku luHoom 'eih?	what meat dishes have you got?

Both **feeh** and **ɛanduku** can be used separately or together.

Examples

feeh kukakoula?	
feeh ɛanduku kukakoula?	Have you got a Coca-Cola?
ɛanduku kukukoula?	

the way it works

Would you like?

When asking an individual or a group what they *would like* (1) or *would like to do* (2) use the following:

(1)	**tiHibb 'ahwa?** (m.)	Would you like coffee?
	tiHibbi 'ahwa walla shaay? (f.)	Would you like coffee or tea?
	tiHibbu ɛeish wi salaTa? (pl.)	Would you like bread and salad?

(2)   **tiHibb tishrab 'eih?** (m.)   What would you like to drink?
       tiHibbu taklu'eih? (pl.)   What would you like to eat?

      Also

(2)   **tiHibbtishrab kukakoula?** (m.)   ⎫
       tiHibbi tishrabi kukakoula? (f.)   ⎬   Would you like to drink
       tiHibbu tishrabu kukakoula? (pl.) ⎭   Coca Cola?

When the enquiry is about food or drink the word **Talab** (s.) or **Talabaat** (pl.) is used with the appropriate pronoun ending.

Examples

Talabak'eih? (m.)	What would you like?	⎫
Talabik'eih? (f.)	What would you like?	⎬ (singular)
Talabku'eih? (pl.)	What would you like?	⎭
Talabaatak'eih? (m.)	What would you like?	⎫
Talabaatik'eih? (f.)	What would you like?	⎬ (plural)
Talabaatku'eih? (pl.)	What would you like?	⎭

tiHibbu tishrabu'eih? or **Talabaatku'eih?** are more polite than **tishrabu'eih?** or **ɛayzeen'eih?**

things to do

6.4   Say the following to the waiter:

1   I have booked a table for two.
2   In the name of (give your name)
3   Can we have the menu please?
4   Can we have something to drink?
5   I would like a table for four.
6   What vegetables have you got?
7   What cold drinks have you got?
8   Have you got Turkish coffee?
9   Have you got rice or macaroni?
10   Have you got okra?

6.5   Order the following dishes and drinks:

1   One lentil soup and three tomato soups.
2   Two Pepsis and two lemon juices.
3   Three kebabs and one kufta.
4   Two coffees with a little sugar.
5   Four mint teas.

TALKING WITH FRIENDS

muHadsa/Making conversation

Bill and Catherine are sitting in the hotel lounge waiting for a friend to come and collect them. A middle-aged man sitting close by strikes up a conversation.

Man:	SabaaH ilkheir, **'intu-mnein**?
Bill:	'iHna **min ingiltira, wi HaDritak** minein?
Man:	**'ana maSri, min 'aSwaan.**
Catherine:	HaDritak **bitishtaghal 'eih**?
Man:	'ana **taagir**.
Bill:	HaDritak **geit ilqaahira 'imta**?
Man:	'ana geit **min yumein**, wintu geitu 'imta?
Catherine:	'iHna geina **min 'usbooε**.
Man:	**wib tiεmilu 'eih hina**?
Bill:	**'iHna SaHafiyyeen. biniktib εan ilbilaad il εarabiyya.**
Man:	**wi 'aεdeen 'add 'eih** fi maSr?
Bill:	**'iHna-msafreen** inniharda.
Man:	**bissalaama. 'ana kamaan misaafir** inniharda.
Catherine:	bissalaama.

Words and phrases from the dialogue

'intu-mnein?	where are you from?
min ingiltira/aSwaan	from England/Aswan
HaDritak (m.)/**HaDritik** (f.)	respectful form of address
'ana maSri (taagir)	I am Egyptian (a merchant)
bitishtaghal 'eih?	what do you do for a living?
geit ilqaahira 'imta?	when did you come to Cairo?
min yumein ('usbooε)	two days (a week) ago
wib tiεmilu 'eih hina?	and what are you doing here?
iHna SaHafiyyeen	we are journalists
biniktib εan	we are writing about
ilbilaad ilεarabiyya	the Arab countries

wi 'aɛdeen 'add 'eih?	and how long are you staying?
'iHna-msafreen	we are travelling/leaving
bissalaama	have a safe journey
'ana kamaan misaafir	I, too, am travelling/leaving

Talking about your occupation

To ask about someone's occupation you can say

inta (HaDritak) bitishtaghal'eih/fein? (m.)
inti (HaDritik) bitishaghali'eih/fein? (f.)
intu-b tishtaghalu'eih/fein? (pl.)

They all mean 'What do you do?' 'Where do you work?'

'eih	what	**fein**	where

You can answer this question in one or two ways

'ana + occupation	I am + occupation
or	
'ana bashtaghal + occupation	I work as a + occupation

Examples

'ana mudarris	I am a teacher
or	
'ana bashtaghal mudarris	I work as a teacher
'ana baghtaghal fi sharika	I work in a firm

The following table shows more examples with different pronouns

	subject	*verb (work)*	*occupation*	
I	**'ana**	**bashtaghal**	**mudarris**	teacher
you	**'inta**	**btishtaghal**	**saHafi**	journalist
you	**'inti**	**btishtaghali**	**duktoura**	doctor
he	**huwwa**	**byishtaghal**	**fi sharika**	in a firm
she	**hiyya**	**btishtaghal**	**fi balad ɛarabi**	in an Arab country
we	**'iHna**	**bnishtaghal**	**muHandiseen**	engineers
you	**'intu**	**btishtaghalu**	**saHafiyyeen**	journalists
they	**humma**	**byishtaghalu**	**mudarriseen**	teachers

'ana bashtaghal	I work		in
,,	**fiS SaHaafa**		in the press (journalism)
,,	**fit tadrees**		in teaching
,,	**fil 'izaaɛa**		in broadcasting
,,	**fit tigaara**		in trading (business)
,,	**fis siyaaHa**		in tourism
,,	**fi bank**		in a bank
,,	**fi sharika**		in a company
,,	**fi sharikit bitroul**		in an oil company
,,	**fi maSnaɛ naseeg**		in a textile factory
,,	**fi balad ɛarabi**		in an Arab country
,,	**fi sifaarit briTanya**		at the British Embassy.

Talking about your stay

'inta geit (maSr) 'imta? (m.)
'inti geiti (maSr) 'imta? (f.)   when did you come to (Egypt)?
'intu geitu (maSr) 'imta? (pl.)

'ana geit (maSr) min yumein   I came to (Egypt) two days ago
'iHna geina (maSr) min yumein   we came to (Egypt) two days ago
'inta 'aaɛid 'add 'eih? (m.)   how long are you staying?
'ana 'aaɛid 'usbooɛ   I am staying for a week
'inti 'aɛda 'add 'eih? (f.)   how long are you staying?
'ana 'aɛda talat-t iyyaam   I am staying for three days
'intu 'aɛdeen 'add 'eih? (pl.)   how long are you staying?
'iHna 'aɛdeen ɛashar-t iyyaam   we are staying for ten days
'inta-msaffir 'imta? (m.)
'inti-msafra 'imta? (f.)   when are you leaving (travelling)?
'intu-msafreen 'imta? (pl.)

'ana-msaafir baɛd 'usbooɛ   I am leaving after (in) a week
'ana-msafra baɛd bukra   I am leaving the day after tomorrow
'iHna-msafreen inniharda   we are leaving today

Summary of the structures used above

	pronoun		arrived	staying	travelling
I	(m.)	'ana	geit	'aaɛid	msaafir
I	(f.)	'ana	geit	'aɛda	msafra
You	(m.)	'inta	geit	'aaɛid	msaafir
You	(f.)	'inti	geiti	'aɛda	msafra
He	(m.)	huwwa	gih	'aaɛid	msaafir
She	(f.)	hiyya	gat	'aɛda	msafra
You	(pl.)	'iHna	geina	'aɛdeen	msafreen
They	(pl.)	humma	gum	'aɛdeen	msafreen

Introducing people

'abilt issayid ibraheem? (m.)
'abilti   „   „   (f.)   have you met Mr Ibrahim?

tiɛraf issayid ibraheem (m.)
tiɛrafi   „   „   (f.)   do you know Mr Ibrahim?

Polite expressions

bissalaama   goodbye, have a safe journey
'ila-l liqaa'   see you again, au revoir
'agaaza saɛeeda   have a nice holiday
'insha'allaah tinbisiT (m.)
      „   tinbisTi (f.)   I hope you will have a nice time
      „   tinbisTu (pl.)

Asking about your country

'inta-mnein? (m.)
'inti-mnein? (f.)   where are you from?
intu-mnein? (pl.)

The answer may be:

'ana ingleezi	I am English
'ana min ingiltira	I am from England
'iHna ingleez	we are English
'iHna min ingiltira	we are from England

Talking about languages

bitikkallim ingleezi? (m.)	do you speak English?
bitikkallimi ingleezi? (f.)	do you speak English?
'aywa bakkallim ingleezi	yes, I speak English
la' bakkallim ɛarabi bass	no, I speak Arabic only

the way it works

The continuous present

bi and **ba** are used with the verb in colloquial Arabic when talking about an action going on at the time of speaking or when reporting facts. Both the sounds **i** and **a** in **bi** and **ba** are lost when they are followed or preceded by **a**, **i** or **u** sounds.

Examples

'ana bakkallim ɛarabi	I speak Arabic
'ana bashtaghal SaHafi	I work as a journalist
Catherine **bitishtaghal SaHafiyya**	Catherine works as a journalist
hiyya-b tilɛab tinis	she plays tennis
wib tiɛmilu 'eih hina?	and what are you doing here?

The loss of **i** sound

The word **min** in **min ein** and the word **misaafir**, **misafra** and **misafreen** all lose their i sound when used after a word ending with a vowel.

Examples

'inta		where are you from? (m.)
'inti	**mnein?**	where are you from? (f.)
'intu		where are you from? (pl.)
'inta msaafir		you are leaving (m.)
'inti msafra		you are leaving (f.)
'intu msafreen		you are leaving (pl.)

The loss of a verb

Questions with the verb **bitiɛmil** in all its forms are normally answered like English without this verb.

Examples

bitiɛmilu'eih?	what do you do/what are you doing?

iHna SaHafiyyeen/mudarriseen	we are journalists/teachers
iHna-b niktib gawabaat	we are writing letters
iHna-bnitfarrag εala-t tilifizyoun	we are watching TV

things to do

7.1 You are invited to a party where you meet Arabic-speaking people. Say the following to them.

1 Ask a middle-aged man what he does for work.
2 Ask a young woman if she speaks English.
3 Say you are a teacher.
4 Say you came to Jeddah a week ago.
5 Say you are leaving tomorrow morning.
6 Ask a young journalist what she writes about.
7 Say you are writing about broadcasting in Egypt.
8 Say you are from England.
9 Ask a middle-aged woman where she is from.
10 Say your husband works at the British Embassy.

ziyaarit il'aSHaab/visiting friends

Bill and Catherine are invited by Kamaal and his wife to their home before their departure from Cairo. They are talking over the meal.

Kamaal:	'ahlan **yaraagil, 'izzayyak** inniharda?
Bill:	**'aHsan kiteer.** mumkin 'aakul kull Haaga.
Kamaal:	'ahlan yakatrin **'izzayyik?**
Catherine:	'anna kwayyisa.
Kamaal:	**'abiltu meen** inniharda?
Bill:	'abilna SaHafiyyeen **min gareedit il'ahraam.**
Catherine:	wana 'abilt SaHafiyya **min magallit il'izaaεa.**
Nadya:	εagabku 'eih fi maSr?
Bill:	**'ilgaww Tabεan.** shams kull youm.
Catherine:	'aywa. **'ilgaww hina gameel.**
Kamaal:	iTTayyaara-s saaεa kaam?

Bill:	'iTTayyaara-s saaεa sitta. laakin **laazim nikoon** fil maTaar issaaεa-rbaεa.
Nadya:	**lissa badri.** issaaεa waHda **dilwa'ti.**
Kamaal:	Tayyib **naakul wi nimshi. 'ana raayiH maεaaku**.

Words and phrases from the dialogue

yaraagil	mate/my friend
izzayyak/izzayyik	how are you (m./f.)
'aHsan kiteer	much better
'abiltu meen	who did you meet?
min gareedit il'ahraam	from 'Al-Ahram' newspaper
min magallit il'izaaεa	from 'Al-Izaεa magazine
εagabku 'eih?	what did you like?
ilgaww Tabεan	the weather of course
shams kull youm	sun every day
ilgaww . . . gameel	the weather . . . is beautiful
laazim nikoon	we must be
lissa badri	there's plenty of time
dilwa'ti	now
naakul wi nimshi	let's go after we eat
ana raayiH maεaaku	I'll go with you

Useful words and phrases

Greetings: Here are some ways of saying 'How are you'?

izzayyak	or	**keif Haalak**	when asking one male
izzayyik	or	**keif Haalik**	when asking one female
izzayyuku	or	**keif Halku**	when asking more than one

You could answer:

kwayyis/bikheir/ilHamdu lillaah	fine, very well
'aHsan	better
'aHsan kiteer	much better

kwayyis has different forms for singular and plural
kwayyis (m.)
kwayyisa (f.)
kwayiseen (pl.)

The other expressions **bikheir** and **ilHamdu lillaah** are used for singular and plural, male and female, without change.

Publications

gareeda/garaayid	newspaper/newspapers
magalla/magallaat	magazine/magazines
kitaab/kutub	book/books

Talking about the weather
When talking about the weather you can use the following expressions:

'iddinya bard/Harr	it is cold/hot
'iddinya bard/Harr giddan	it is very cold/hot
'ilgaww bard/Harr	it is cold/hot

'ilgaww bard/Harr giddan	it is very cold/hot
'ishshams TalƐa	the sun is shining
'iddinya Dalma/noor	it is dark/light
'iddinya bitmaTTar	it is raining
'ilgaww gameel/kwayyis	it (the weather) is beautiful/fine

'iddinya literally means the world and 'ilgaww means the weather.

Early and late

dilw'ati	now	Haalan	immediately
bisurƐa	quickly	lissa badri	there's plenty of time
baƐdein	later	mit'akhkhar	late
badri	early		

the way it works

Changes in pronunciation

issaaƐa loses its (i) sound when you say iTTayyaara-s saaƐa kaam because of the final a in iTTayyaara.

gareedit and magallit
Like feminine words ending with a'gareeda and magalla become gareedit and magallit when followed by their names, or any other noun.

gareedit il'ahraam	'Al-Ahram' newspaper
magallit il'izaaƐa	'Al-IzaƐa' magazine
gareedit kamaal	Kamaal's newspaper
magallit ishshahrida	this month's magazine

The same applies to ziyaara which becomes ziyaarit when followed by il'aSHaab.

laazim amshi/akoon = must go/be

These verbs change form according to the subject.

pronoun		must go	must be
(I)	'ana	laazim amshi	laazim akoon
(you)	'inta (m.)	laazim timshi	laazim tikoon
(you)	'inti (f.)	laazim timshi	laazim tikooni
(he)	huwwa	laazim yimshi	laazim yikoon
(she)	hiyya	laazim timshi	laazim tikoon
(we)	'iHna	laazim nimshi	laazim nikoon
(you)	'intu (pl.)	laazim timshu	laazim tikoonu
(they)	humma	laazim yimshu	laazim yikoonu

things to do

7.2 Can you reply in Arabic to the speaker?

	Speaker:	**'izzayyak?**
1	you:	very well, thank you.
	Speaker:	**'abilt meen inniharda?**
2	you:	I met a writer from Lebanon.
	Speaker:	**hatrooH ilmaTaar 'imta?**
3	you:	I must be at the airport at 7 o'clock.
	Speaker:	**'ana mumkin aroolt maɛaak.**
4	you:	Thank you. When can we go?
	Speaker:	**ɛaayiz garaayid aw magallaat?**
5	you:	yes, 'AL-Ahram' please.

bissalaama/Have a safe journey

Kamaal and Nadya are saying goodbye to Bill and Catherine at the airport.

Kamaal:	tishrabu 'ahwa walla shaay?
Catherine:	'ana ashrab 'ahwa maZbooT.
Bill:	wana kamaan 'ahwa maZbooT.
Nadya:	**'ismaɛ ya Kamaal biynaadu ɛala-r rukkaab**
Kamaal:	**doul biynaadu ɛala rukkaab rouma.**
Nadya:	**'aywa SaHeeH. laazim tiktibulna** min ingiltira
Catherine:	Tabɛan, **wintu laazim teegu ingiltira**
Kamaal:	**'uraayib insha'allah**
Bill:	dilwa'ti **biynaadu ɛaleina**
Nadya:	'aywa SaHeeH. itfaDDalu intu. bissalaama
Catherine:	salaam ya nadya, **mutshakkireen giddan**
Bill:	salaamu ɛaleikum. nishufku f-ingiltira
Kamaal:	maɛassalaama, maɛassalaama.

Words and phrases from the dialogue

'ismaɛ ya Kamaal	listen Kamaal
biynaadu ɛala-r rukkab	they are calling the passengers
doul biynaadu ɛala	they are calling
rukkaab rouma	Rome passengers
'aywa SaHeeH	yes, that's true
laazim tiktibulna	you must write to us
wintu laazim teegu ingiltira	and you must come to England.
'urayyib insha'allah	soon, God willing
biynaadu ɛaleina	they are calling us
mutshakkireen giddan	many thanks

the way it works

'urayyib means 'near', in time and place.

'insh'allah means 'God willing'. This expression is used by most Arabs when talking about anything happening in the future.

doul originally means **these**, but it is also used in some cases to mean **they**, as in the sentence in the dialogue, **doul biynaadu ɛala rukkaab rouma**.

mutshakkireen is the plural of **mutshakkir** (m.) and **mutshakkira** (f.) which mean 'thank you'.

things to do

7.3 You are saying goodbye to your friends at the airport. Say in Arabic:

1. Who are these people?
2. They are passengers for Paris.
3. Listen (m. + f. pl.).
4. They are calling us.
5. What's the time now?
6. Robert, you must write to me.
7. And you must write to me, my friend.
8. Have a safe journey, Nadya.
9. See you (Salem) in London.
10. Soon, God willing.

1.1 1 'ahlan/'ahlan wa sahlan
2 furSa saɛeeda 3 'ana Sally 4 da-zmeeli Tom 5 'ana 'aHmad 6 di zugti nadya 7 'irriHla kannit kwayyisa?
8 'aywa irriHla kaanit kwayyisa giddan. 9 fein iɛarabiyya?/iɛarabiyya fein? 10 iɛarabiyya fil maw'af.
1.2 1 'anna ɛandi Hagz hina 2 ismi Bill Taylor. 3 ɛaayiz 'ouDa-b dushsh, min faDlik. 4 bikaam illeila?
5 'ilmaTɛam fein, min faDlik?
1.3 1 ɛandak 'ouDa faDya? 2 la', 'ana ɛayza 'ouDa-b Hammaam.
3 'arbaɛ layaali, min faDlak.
4 mumkin ilmuftaaH, min faDlak?
5 il'ouDa fein, min faDlak?

2.1 1 ɛandak éih? (feeh éih?)
2 ɛandak (feeh) mirabbit éih?
3 takhdi shaay? (tishrabi . . . ?)
4 takhdi ɛaSeer? 5 taakul éih?
6 tishrab éih? 7 'aakhud fool wi gibna wi-mrabbit balaH. 8 y'aakhud 'ahwa-b laban.
2.2 1 talaata (sandwitsh) falaafil.
2 itnein (sandwitsh) gibna. 3 'arbaɛa ɛaSeer burtu'aan. 4 waaHid (sandwitsh) fool. 5 sitta bibsi.
6 khamsa ɛaSeer lamoon.
2.3 1 mumkin 'aghayyar istirleeni hina? 2 ilgineih il'istrleeni-b kaam?
3 mumkin 'aghayyar shikaat siyaHiyya? 4 la', dularaat. 5 miyya itnein wi talateen dulaar.
2.4 1 feeh kaam 'ouDa fil huteil? 2 It has sixty-five rooms. 3 bikaam il'ouDa-l shakhS waaHid? 4 It is forty-five pounds per night. 5 feeh bank fil huteil? 6 Yes, there is. 7 mumkin 'aghayyar ɛumla hina? 8 What do you want to change? 9 ɛaayiz aghayyar dularaat. 10 You can, of course.
2.5 1 'ilfiTaar issaaɛa kaam?
2 issaaɛa sabɛa-w nuSS. 3 il'akHbaar issaaɛa kaam? 4 issaaɛa khamsa
5 mumkin atɛashsha-s saaɛa kaam?
6 min issaaɛa sabɛa lissaaɛa tamanya-w nuSS. 7 issaaɛa kaam dilwa'ti?
8 issaaɛa sitta. 9 issaaɛa dilwa'ti tamanya-lla rubɛ? 10 la', issaaɛa dilwa'ti tamanya-w rubɛ.

3.1 1 fein 'a'rab agzakhaana?
2 'arrooH maktab ilbareed izzaay?
3 fein 'ism ilbulees (ishshurTa)?
4 feeh bi'aala 'urayyiba min hina?
5 'arooH maHTTit il'aTr izzaay?
3.2 1 'imshi-f shaariɛ ibraheem liHadd midaan ramsees, wi baɛdein Hawwid yimeen fi shaariɛ ramsees wimshi-l Hadd shaariɛ issalaam, ilbank ɛala-n naSya. 2 'imshi-f shaariɛ ramsees liHadd shaariɛ shubra, wibaɛdein Hawwid yimeen wimshi-l Hadd shaariɛ luxor, maktab ilbareed 'awwil mabna ɛala-l yimeen. 3 imshi-f shaariɛ luxor liHadd shaariɛ ibraheem, wibaɛdein Hawwid yimeen wimshi-f shaariɛ ibraheem liHadd midaan ramsees. 'ism ilbulees hinaak fil midaan.
4 'idkhul fi shaariɛ ibraheem fittigaah shaariɛ luxor, wibaɛdein Hawwid yimeen fi shaariɛ luxor. taalit dukkaan ɛala-l yimeen huwwa-l maktaba.
5 'imshi-f shaariɛ luxor fittigaah shaariɛ ibraheem, wibaɛdein Hawwid shimaal fi shaariɛ ibraheem wimshi-l Hadd ilmidaan. ilmatHaf 'awwil mabna ɛala-l yimeen.
3.3 1 'arooH issook izzaay?
2 mumkin naakhud taksi min hina?
3 'utubees nimra kaam biyrooH maSr iggideeda? 4 nighayyar fein? 5 fein figgeeza?
3.4 ɛayza arooH huteil il'andalus.
2 laazim takhdi taksi. 3 Clare mumkin taakhud 'utubees. 4 feeh 'utubees ɛalaTool? 5 la' laazim tighayyari-f baab ilHadeed. 6 fein maw'af il'utubees? 7 'uddaam ilbank.
8 ittazkara-b kaam? 9 ittazkara-b ɛishreen 'irsh. 10 kwayyis giddan.
3.5 1 ɛaayiz arooH il'azhar.
2 'il'azhar gaamiɛ 'adeem. 3 khaan ilkhaleeli sou' kibeer. 4 mumkin 'ashoof 'eih fil matHaf? 5 nirooH khaan ilkhaleeli izzaay? 6 ɛaayiz ashoof gaamiɛ gideed. 7 iddukkaan da-Sghayyar giddan.

4.1 1 keelu-l manga-b kaam? (bikaam keelu-l manga?) 2 keelu-l farawla-b kaam? (bikaam keelu-l farawla?) 3 'ijjakitta alkhaDra-b kaam?

KEY TO EXERCISES

(bikaam . . . ?) 4 il'ameeS ilbeij bikaam . . .? (bikaam . . . ?) 5 ittimsaal da-b kaam? (bikaam . . . ?)

4.2 1 la' di ghalya kida. 2 Tayyib iddeeni sitt kroot. 3 'aakhud ilgamal il 'aHmar. 4 'aakhud talat galaleeb. 5 'aadi khamsa gneih wi haat ilbaa'i.

4.3 1 εaayiz/εayza abεat ilkuroot di birmingham. 2 mumkin abεat ilgawaab da musaggal, min faDlak? 3 mumkin abεat iTTurood di barees, min faDlak? 4 εaayiz/εayza Taabiε lilkart da min faDlak. 5 εaayiz/εayza abεat ilgawabaat di bil bareed ilgawwi. εaayiz/εayza abεat ilgawabaat di biTTayyaara. 6 fein waSl ittasgeel? 7 bikaam iTTaabiε libriTanya bareed gawwi? bikaam iTTaabiε libriTanya biTTayyaara? 8 mumkin astaεmil ittilifoun? 9 mumkin akallim iskindiriyya? 10 εaayiz/εayza akallim manshistar, min faDlak.

5.1 1 'aTr lukSur issaaεa kaam? 2 iHna-msafreen youm iggumεa-S SubH. 3 εaayiz aHgiz 'arbaε amaakin, min faDlak. 4 daraga 'oola mukayyafa. 5 iHna rayHeen bil'aTr-iw ragεeen biTTayyaara. 6 mumkin aHgiz diwaan bisrireîn? 7 bikaam ittazkara? 8 feeh εarabiyyit 'akl? 9 il'aTr iy'oom issaaεa kaam? 10 wi yiwSal issaaεa kaam?

5.2 1 'ana εayza aHgiz makaan lijidda. 2 iHna-msafra youm iggumεa baεd iDDuhr. 3 bikaam ittazkara raayiH gayy? 4 daraga siyaHiyya. 5 iTTayyaara-t'oom issaaεa kaam? 6 iTTayyaara tiwSal jidda-s saaεa kaam?

5.3 1 mumkin aHgiz malεab iskwaash? 2 'add'eih? 3 saaεa (waHda). 4 εaayiz maDaarib? 5 la' εandina maDaarib. 6 khamsa-gneih min faDlak. 7 mumkin nilεab imta? 8 'issaaεa arbaεa-w nuSS. 9 feeh dushsh hina? 10 'aywa, feeh talaata. 11 humma fein? 12 fi 'aakhir ilmamarr da, εala-sh shimaal.

5.4 1 feeh 'eih? 2 wi feeh 'eih kamaan? 3 sahrit ilhuteil feeha 'eih? 4 wi sahrit innaadi feeha 'eih? 5 Tayyib. nirooH innadi illilaadi.

6.1 1 Tom sinaanu-b tiwgaεu. 2 Laura εandaha bard. 3 Josephine εandaha iltihaab fi zurha. 4 Helen εinha-b tiwgaεha. 5 Henry εandu HumooDa.

6.2 1 Have you got a cold? la' maεandeesh. 2 Have you got a temperature? 'aywa (εandi) 3 Are you allergic to penicillin? la' maεandeesh. 4 Since when? min inniharda-S SubH. 5 Have you got a headache? (Is there a headache?) la' mafeesh.

6.3 1 feeh Haaga liSSudaaε, min faDlak? 2 mumkin aSrif irrushitta di? 3 εaayiz maεgoon Hilaa'a-w maεgoon 'asnaan. 4 εaayiz 'uTn Tibbi-w detoul wi 'ilastublast. 5 εaayiz Haaga lil is-haal wi muTahhir. 6 'aakhud iddawa da kaam marra? 7 'aakhud 'add 'éih? 8 furshit 'asnaan min faDlak. 9 kulunya-w budra min faDlak. 10 furshit Hilaa'a-w amwaas min faDlak.
* (Words can be changed to fit masculine or femine speaker or pharmacist. e.g. εaayiz – εayza, min faDlak – min faDlik.)

6.4 1 'ana Haagiz (Hagza) tarabeiza litnein. 2 bism (give your name). 3 mumkin ilminyu, min faDlak? 4 mumkin nishrab Haaga? 5 εaayiz (εayza) tarabeiza larbaεa. 6 εandak khuDaar 'eih? 7 εandak 'eih saa'iε? 8 feeh (εandak) 'ahwa turki? 9 feeh (εandak) ruzz aw makarouna? 10 feeh (εandak) bamya?

6.5 1 waaHid shurbit εats wi talaata shurbit TamaaTim. 2 itnein bibsi witnein εaSeer lamoon. 3 talaata kabaab wiwaaHid kufta. 4 itnein 'ahwa maZbooT. 5 'arbaεa shaay biniεnaaε.

7.1 1 HaDritak bitishtaghal éih?
2   bitikkallimi ingleezi? 3 'ana
mudarris (mudarrisa). 4 'ana waSalt
(geit) jidda min 'usbooε. 5 'ana-msaafir
bukra-S SubH. 6   bitiktibi εan 'eih?
7 'ana baktib εan il'izaaεa-f maSr.
8 'ana min ingiltira. 9 HaDritik min
ein? 10   zougi-b yishtaghal fissifaara-l
briTaniyya.
7.2 1 'ana kwayyis, shukran. 2 'abilt
kaatib min libnaan. 3   laazim akoon

filmaTaar issaaεa sabεa. 4   shukran.
mumkin nimshi 'imta? 5 'aywa, 'il
'ahram min faDlak.
7.3 1   doul meen (meen doul)?
2   doul rukkaab Parees. 3 'ismaεu ya
gamaaεa. 4   bynaadu εaleina.
5   issaaεa kaam dilwa'ti? 6   laazim
tiktibli yaRobert. 7   winta laazim tiktibli
yaraagil. 8   bissalaama ya nadya.
9 'ashoofak fi landan. 10 'urayyib,
inshaa'allah.

VOCABULARY

ENGLISH–ARABIC
TOPIC VOCABULARIES

Numbers

Cardinal numbers 1–10

Numbers for time, money and orders		*Numbers for other items*	
1	**waaHid** (m.)	1	**waaHid** (m.)
1	**waHda** (f.)	1	**waHda** (f.)
2	**'itnein**	2	**'itnein**
3	**talaata**	3	**talat**
4	**'arbaɛa**	4	**'arbaɛ**
5	**khamsa**	5	**khamas**
6	**sitta**	6	**sitt**
7	**sabɛa**	7	**sabaɛ**
8	**tamanya**	8	**taman**
9	**tisɛa**	9	**tisaɛ**
10	**ɛashara**	10	**ɛashar**

Cardinal numbers 11–30 (for all purposes)

11	**HiDaashar**	18	**tamanTaashar**	25	**khamsa-w ɛishreen**
12	**'itnaashar**	19	**tisaɛTaashar**	26	**sitta-w ɛishreen**
13	**talaTTaashar**	20	**ɛishreen**	27	**sabɛa-w ɛishreen**
14	**'arbaɛTaashar**	21	**waaHid wi ɛishreen**	28	**tamanya-w ɛishreen**
15	**khamasTaashar**	22	**'itnein wi ɛishreen**	29	**tisɛa-w ɛishreen**
16	**siTTaashar**	23	**talaata-w ɛishreen**	30	**talateen**
17	**sabɛTaashar**	24	**'arbaɛ-w ɛishreen**		

Cardinal numbers 40–1000

40	**'arbiɛeen**	100	**miyya (meet)**	700	**subɛumiyya**
50	**khamseen**	200	**mitein**	800	**tumnumiyya**
60	**sitteen**	300	**tultumiyya**	900	**tusɛumiyya**
70	**sabɛeen**	400	**rubɛumiyya**	1000	**'alf**
80	**tamaneen**	500	**khumsumiyya**		
90	**tisɛeen**	600	**suttumiyya**		

Ordinal numbers 1st–10th

Indefinite (m. & f.)		*Definite* (the . . .)	
		(m.)	(f.)
1st	**'awwil**	**'il'awwal**	**'il'oola**
2nd	**taani**	**'ittaani**	**'ittanya**
3rd	**taalit**	**'ittaalit**	**'ittalta**
4th	**raabiɛ**	**'irraabiɛ**	**'irrabɛa**
5th	**khaamis**	**'ilkhaamis**	**'ilkhamsa**
6th	**saadis**	**'issaadis**	**'issadsa**
7th	**saabiɛ**	**'issaabiɛ**	**'issabɛa**
8th	**taamin**	**'ittaamin**	**'ittamna**
9th	**taasiɛ**	**'ittaassiɛ**	**'ittasɛa**
10th	**ɛaashir**	**'ilɛaashir**	**'ilɛashra**

Time

second	sanya	week	'usbooɛ
minute	di'ee'a	month	shahr
hour	saaɛa	year	sana
day	youm		
today	'inniharda/'ilyoum	tomorrow	bukra/baakir
yesterday	'imbariH/'ams	every day	kull youm
two days ago	min yumein	in two days time	baɛd yumein
two weeks ago	min 'usbuɛein	in two weeks time	baɛd 'sbuɛein
last week	il'usbooɛ ilmaaDi	next week	il'usbooɛ ilgaay
in the morning	'iSSubH	at noon	'iDDuhr
in the afternoon	baɛd iDDuhr	in the evening	fil masaa'
		at night	bil leil

Months of the year/shuhoor issana

January	yanaayir	July	yulya
February	fibraayir	August	aghusTus
March	maaris	September	sibtambir
April	'abreel	October	'uktoubar
May	maayu	November	noufambir
June	yunya	December	deesambir

Clothes

Arab loose costume	galabiyya	kaftan	'ufTaan
blouse	bilouza	overcoat	balTu
dress	fustaan	shirt	'ameeS
for boys	lil'awlaad	slippers	shibshib
for girls	banaati	socks	sharaab
for men	rigaali	suit (for men)	badla
for women	Hareemi	suit (for women)	taiyeir
handbag	shanTit yadd	shoes	gazma
jacket	jakitta	trousers	banTaloun

Sizes

small size	ma'aas Sughayyar
medium size	ma'aas mutawassiT
large size	ma'aas kibeer
one size	ma'aas waaHid

Colours

	(m.)	(f.)		(m.)	(f.)
beige	beij	beij	green	'akhDar	khaDra
black	'iswid	souda	red	'aHmar	Hamra
blue	'azra'	zar'a	white	'abyaD	beiDa
brown	bunni	bunni	yellow	'asfar	Safra

VOCABULARY

Space

near	'urayyib/'areeb	far	biɛeed
right	yimeen	left	shimaal
in front of	'udddaam/amaam	behind	wara/khalf

Food

Fruit

apples	tuffaaH	melons	shammaam
apricots	mishmish	oranges	burtu'aan
bananas	mouz	peaches	khoukh
dates	balaH/tamr	pears	kummitra
figs	teen	plums	bar'oo'
grapes	ɛinab	strawberries	farawla
mangoes	manga	water melons	baTTeekh

Vegetables

aubergine	bidingaan	green beans	faSulya
cabbage	kurunb	lettuce	khaSS
carrots	gazar	okra	bamya
courgettes	kousa	onions	baSal
cucumber	'atta	peas	bisilla
garlic	toum	potatoes	baTaaTis
gherkins	khiyaar	tomatoes	TamaaTim

Drinks

coffee	'ahwa
coffee with milk	'ahwa-b laban
Turkish coffee (without sugar)	'ahwa saada
(with little sugar)	'ahwa maZbooT
(with lots of sugar)	'ahwa zyaada (ziyaada)
tea with milk	shaay bilaban
black tea	shaay saada
cold drink	Haaga sa'ɛa
juice	ɛaSeer
,, banana	,, mouz
,, mango	,, manga
,, orange	,, burtu'aan
,, strawberry	,, farawla
mineral water	maiya maɛdaniyya
beer	beera
wine	nibeet

Miscellaneous

bread	ɛeish/khubz
French bread	ɛeish feenu
local bread	ɛeish baladi
cheese	gibna
cooked broad beans (Egyptian)	fool midammis

egg/eggs	beiDa/beiD
bean burgers	falaafil
fish	samak
gateau	gatou
jam	mirabba
fig jam	mirabbit teen
kebab	kabaab
macaroni	makarouna
meat	laHm/laHma
oriental cakes	Halawiyaat shar'iya
pancake/s	fiTeera/fiTeer
pepper	filfil
rice	ruzz
salad	SalaTa
salt	malH/milH
sandwich	sandawitsh
soup	shurba
lentil soup	shurbit ɛats
sugar	sukkar
Turkish delight	malban

Cooking methods

boiled	**masloo'**	grilled	**mashwi**
fried	**ma'li/miHammar**	roasted	**ruSTu**

Meals

breakfast	**'ilfiTaar**	supper	**'ilɛasha**
lunch	**'ilghada**		

At the chemist's

the pharmacy	**'iS-Saidaliya/'il'agzakhaana**
the chemist	**'iS-Saidali** (m.)/**'iS-Saidaliya** (f.)
after-shave	**kulunya-l baɛd il Hilaa'a**
aspirin	**'aspireen**
brush	**fursha**
hair brush	**furshit shaɛr**
shaving brush	**furshit Hilaa'a**
toothbrush	**furshit sinaan ('asnaan)**
condoms	**kababeet**
cotton wool	**'uTn Tibbi**
Dettol	**ditoul**
disinfectant/antiseptic	**muTahhir**
laxative	**mulayyin (dawa mulayyin)**
medicine for …	**dawa li …**
pain killer	**musakkin (dawa musakkin)**
razor blades	**'amwaas Hilaa'a**
sanitary towels (women's)	**fiwaT (HifaDaat) nisa'iya**
shaving cream	**maɛgoon (kreim) Hilaa'a**
soap (for the bath)	**Saaboon Hammaam**

VOCABULARY

syringe/injection	Hu'na
syringes/injections	Hu'an
tablets/pills	'urS (s.)/a'raaS (pl.)
toothpaste	maɛgoon sinaan ('asnaan)

Ailments

cold	bard	heartburn	HumooDa
constipation	imsaak	sore . . .	iltihaab fi . . .
cough	kuHHa	stomach-ache	maghaS
diarrhoea	is-haal	temperature	Haraara
headache	Sudaaɛ	vomiting	qei'

Parts of the body

arm	diraaɛ	leg	rigl
chest	sidr/Sadr	mouth	bu'/famm
ear	widn	nose	manakheer
eye	ɛein	shoulder	kitf
finger	Subaaɛ	stomach	baTn
fingers	Sawaabiɛ	teeth	sinaan/'asnaan
foot	'adam/rigl	tongue	lisaan
hand	'eed/yad	toe	Subaaɛ rigl
head	raaS	tooth	sinna

Leisure

antiquities	'asaar	night club	kazinu/naadi layli
booking	Hagz	play (n.)	masraHiya
café	'ahwa	programme	birnaamig
church	kineesa	pyramid	haram
cinema	sinama	The Pyramids	'il'ahraam
dancing	ra'S	son et lumière	'iSSouT wiDDou'
evening entertainment	sahra	songs	'aghaani
mosque	gaamiɛ	temple	maɛbad
museum	matHaf	theatre	masraH
music	museeqa	ticket	tazkara

Sport

ball	koura	entrance fee	rasm-idkhool
. . . ball	kourit . . .	game	liɛba
bat	maDrab	hire	ta'geer
club	naadi	match	mubaraa
court	malɛab	racket	maDrab
squash	iskwash	table tennis	bing bung
sunbathing	Hammam shams	table tennis bat	maDrab bing bung
swimming	sibaaHa/ɛoum	tennis	tinis
swimming pool	Hammam sibaaHa	tennis ball	kourit tinis
table	tarabeiza	tennis racket	maDrab tinis

VOCABULARY

Occupations

	(m.)	(f.)
accountant	muHaasib	muHaasiba
author	mu'allif/kaatib	mu'allifa/kaatiba
businessman	ragul 'aɛmaal	
businesswoman		sayyidat 'aɛmaal
diplomat	diblumaasi	diblumasiyya
doctor	doktour/Tabeeb	doktoura/Tabeeba
engineer	muhandis	muhandisa
journalist	SaHafi	SaHafiyya
lawyer	muHaami	muHamiya
manager	mudeer	mudeera
nurse	mumarriD	mumarriDa
police officer	DaabiT bulees	
secretary	sikirteir	sikirteira
teacher	mudarris	mudarrisa
writer	kaatib/mu'allif	kaatiba/mu'allifa

Useful words and phrases

Essential expressions

Greetings

Good morning	SabaaH ilkheir
	SabaaH innoor
Good afternoon/evening	masaa' ilkheir
	masaa' innoor
Goodnight	tiSbaH ɛalakheir
Hello	ahlan/marHaba
Pleased to meet you	furSa saɛeeda
Where is . . . ?	fein . . . ?
the telephone?	ittilifoun?
the toilet?	ilHammam? (ittiwalitt)
the bathroom?	ilHammam?
the post office?	maktab ilbareed?
the police station?	'ism ilbulees?
would like/would like to/need	ɛaayiz (m.) ɛayza (f.) ɛayeen (pl.)
I would like to go to the club	ɛaayiz arooH innaadi (m.)
	ɛayza arooH innaadi (f.)
we would like to go to the club	ɛayzeen nirooH innadi
can and cannot	mumkin and mish mumkin
can I see the manager?	mumkin ashoof ilmudeer?
yes, you can	'aywa mumkin
no, you cannot	la' mish mumkin
must, have to	laazim
and do not have to	mish laazim
I must leave tomorrow.	laazim amshi bukra

VOCABULARY

you have to book a seat.	**laazim tiHgiz makaan**
you don't have to change money.	**mish laazim tighayyar fuloos/ɛumla**

In the airport

arrival	**wuSool**
departure	**safar**
entry visa	**ta'sheerit dukhool**
exit visa	**ta'sheerit khuroog**
flight no.	**riHla raqam**
gate	**bawwaaba**
lounge/hall (departure lounge)	**saala (saalit ... issafar)**
passenger	**raakib** (m.) **rakba** (f.)
passengers	**rukkaab**
passport	**basbour/gawaaz**
passports	**basburtaat/gawazaat**

VOCABULARY

ARABIC–ENGLISH VOCABULARY

'a'rab nearest
'aadi here is (are)
aakhud I (I'll) take
aakul I (I'll) eat
'aasif I am sorry
abɛat I send
'abl before
'abilt I met
'abyaD white
'adam foot
'add 'eih how much (many)?
'adeem old/ancient
'agaaza holiday
aghayyar I (I'll) change
'agzakhaana pharmacy
'ahlan Hello!
'ahlan wa sahlan Hello!
'ahwa café, coffee
aHDar I (I'll) attend
'aHmar red
'aHsan better
akallim speak to
akkallim fi use (the phone)
'akbar bigger
'akhDar green
'akl food
aktib I (I'll) write
alɛab I (I'll) play
'alf one thousand
'alou Hello! (on phone)
amDi I (I'll) sign
'amreeki/ya American (m./f.)
amshi I (I'll) walk
'ana I (1st person)
'araSni (m.) bit/stung me (wasp)
'araSitni (f.) bit/stung me (bee)
arbaɛ/arbaɛa four
arbaɛTaashar fourteen
arbiɛeen forty
'arkhaS cheaper
arooH I (I'll) go
'aSanseir lift
'aSfar yellow
aSrif cash
asaafir I (I'll) travel
'asbaani Spanish
asmaɛ I (I'll) hear
astaɛmil I (I'll) use
ashoof I (I'll) see
ashrab I (I'll) drink

ashtiri I (I'll) buy
atfarrag I (I'll) watch
'aTr train
'awwal/'awwil (adj.) first
'awwalan (adv.) first
'aywa yes
'ayy any
'ayyi khidma at your service
'azra' blue

ɛaayiz/ɛayza I want (m./f.)
ɛagabni I liked
ɛala on
ɛala Tool straight on
ɛammaan Amman
ɛan about
ɛand near (adv.)
ɛandi I have
ɛandina we have
ɛarab Arabs
ɛarabiyya car
ɛaSeer juice
ɛashara ten
ɛein eye
ɛilba can/box
ɛishreen twenty
ɛumaan Oman

baɛd after
baɛd iDDuhr in the afternoon
balad country/town
baladi local
bank bank
bansyoun boarding house
banTaloun trousers
bard cold
bareed post/mail
basbour passport
baseeTa not serious
bass only/enough
bastilya pastilles
baSal onions
baTaaTis potatoes
baTn stomach
beera beer
beiDa egg (white, f.)
beij beige
beit house
beit shabaab youth hostel

86

VOCABULARY

bi with/by/at
bidingaan aubergine
biɛeed/a far away (m./f.)
bikaam for how much?
billeil at night
bilouza blouse
bint girl
bisilla peas
bissalaama goodbye
bisurɛa quickly
bu' mouth
budra powder
bukra tomorrow
bunni brown
burtu'aan oranges

da this (m.)
daakhil inside
dabboor wasp
daraga class (transport)
dawa medicine
di this (f.)
diblumaasi/ya diplomat (m./f.)
di'ee'a minute (1/60 hour)
dinaar dinar (currency)
diraaɛ arm (body)
dirham currency
ditoul Dettol
diwaan compartment (train)
doul these/those
dour floor
dukkaan shop
duktour doctor
dulaar dollar
dushsh shower

'eed hand (body)
'eih? what?

faaDi vacant/free
falaafil bean burgers
farawla strawberries
faSulya green beans
fatoora bill
feeh . . . ? is/are there?
fein . . . ? where is?
fi in
film film
fiTaar (il-) breakfast
fool midammis cooked broad beans
fuloos money
funduq hotel
furSa saɛeeda pleased to meet you!

fursha brush
furshit . . .   . . . brush

gaamiɛ mosque
galabiyya loose Arab costume
gamal camel
ganb beside
gatou gateau
gawaab letter
gawaafa guava
gaww weather
gazar carrots
gazma shoes (pair)
geit I arrived
gibna cheese
giddan very

ghaali/ghalya expensive (m./f.)
ghada (il-) lunch

haat give me
haram pyramid
hina here
hinaak there
hiyya she
humma they
huteil hotel
huwwa he

HaaDir yes/certainly
Haaga thing
Haaga tanya anything else?
Haalan in a minute!
Haamil pregnant
Hafla party
Hagz reservation
Hammam bathroom
Hammam sibaaha swimming pool
Hamra red (f.)
Haraara temperature
Hasasiya allergy
Hawwid turn (verb)
HifaDaat nisa'iyya sanitary towels
Hilaa'a shaving
Hilw/Hilwa sweet, beautiful
ilHilw dessert
Hisaab arithmetic
ilHisaab the bill

iddeeni give me
iddinya bard it is cold
iDDuhr at noon
iHna we

VOCABULARY

il the
ilɛafw it's a pleasure
iltihaab inflammation
imbaariH yesterday
imDi sign
imshi walk/go
imta when
inniharda today
inshaa'allah hopefully
inta you (m.)
inti you (f.)
intu you (pl.)
'irsh piastre
'isɛaaf ambulance
'is-haal diarrhoea
'ism name
'ism ilbulees police station
'ismaɛ listen!
issaaɛa . . . it's . . . o'clock
istiqbaal reception
istirleeni sterling
'iswid black
iSSubH in the morning
itfaDDal please/after you
itnaashar twelve
itnein two
'izzaay? how?
'izzaayyak? how are you? (m.)
'izzayyik? how are you? (f.)
'izaaza bottle
'izaazit . . . a bottle of . . .

jakitta jacket

kaam how many?
kaatib writer
kababeet condoms
kabeena cabin/booth
kamaan also/too
kart card
kart bustaal post card
kasart I broke
kibeer large/big
kida like that
kifaaya enough
keelu kilo
kineesa church
kitaab book
kiteer much/a lot
kitf shoulder
koura ball
kourit tinis tennis ball

kreim . . .   . . . cream
kuHHa cough
kul eat
kull . . . every/each
kulunya eau de cologne
kummitra pears
kuroot cards
kwayyis/a good (m.f.)

khaarig outside
khalaaS it's over!
khamas five (things)
khamas Taashar fifteen
khamsa five
khamseen fifty
khareeTa map
khazeena cash desk
kheir good
khoukh peaches
khubz bread
khud take
khuDaar vegetables
khuroog exit

la' no!
laazim must/have to
lamoon lemon/lime
laweit I twisted
leila night
li to/for
liɛba game/toy
lissa not yet

ma'aas size
maɛa with
maɛassalaama goodbye
maɛbad temple
maɛla'a spoon
maɛgoon . . .   . . . paste
mabna building
maDrab racket/bat
mafeesh there isn't
maggaanan free (gratis)
maHaTTa station
makaan (amaakin) seat
maktaba (maktabaat) library/stationers
malH salt
malɛab (malaaɛib) court (sport)
mamarr (mamarrat) corridor
manakheer nose
manzar (manaazir) view
marra (marraat) one time
masaa' evening

VOCABULARY

masaa'ilkheir good evening!
mashwi grilled
masraH theatre
masraHiya play (n.)
maSnaε factory
maSr Egypt/Cairo
maSr iggideeda Heliopolis
maSr il'adeema Old Cairo
matHaf museum
maTaar airport
maw'af . . .   . . . stop
mayya water
maZbooT just right
meet . . . one hundred . . .
midaan square, place
min from
min faDlak please! (m.)
min faDlik please! (f.)
minyu menu
mirabba jam (food)
mirabbit . . .   . . . jam
mish . . . not . . .
mish mumkin you can't
mitein two hundred
mitru metro
miyya one hundred
moos (amwaas) razor blade
mudarris/a teacher
mudeer/a manager
muftaaH key
muhandis/a engineer
mukalma phone call
mulayyin laxative
musaggal recorded
musakkin pain killer
museeqa music
mutashakkir/a thank you
muTahhir antiseptic

naadi club
naadi layli nightclub
nihaar day
nimra number (No.)
nibeet wine
nuSS half

'oola first (f.)
'ouDa room

ra'S dancing
raabiε fourth
raagil (riggaala) man
raaHa rest

raaHa kamla complete rest
raakib (rukkaab) passenger
raas head (body)
raayiH one way/going
raayiH gayy return
rabw asthma
ragul acmaal businessman
ramaDaan fasting month
raSeef platform
rigl leg/foot
riHla trip/flight
rikheeS cheap
riyaaDa sport
rubε a quarter
rushitta prescription
ruzz rice

sa'εa cold
saabiε seventh
saaεa hour/clock
saεeed/a happy/pleased
sabεa, sabaε seven
sabaεTaashar seventeen
sabεeen seventy
sahra evening entertainment
salaam peace!/bye!
samak fish
sana year
sandawitsh sandwich
sandoo' box
sandoo' bareed post box
sanya second (1/60 minute)
sayyid Mr
sayyida Mrs/lady
sidr chest
sifaara embassy
sinama cinema
sinna (sinaan) teeth
sireer bed
sitt woman/lady
sitt/sitta six
sitteen sixty
siTTaashar sixteen
sook, soo' market
suttumiyya six hundred

SabaaH morning
SabaaH ilkheir good morning
Saboon soap
SaHafi/yya journalist (m./f.)
Saniyya tray
Sarraf cashier
Subaaε finger

89

VOCABULARY

Subaaε rigl toe
Sudaaε headache
Sughayyar small

shaariε street
shaay tea
shaεbi folk/popular
shakhS (ashkhaaS) person
shanTa (shunaT) bag/suitcase
sharika (sharikaat) firm/company
sheek (shikaat) cheque
sheek siyaaHi traveller's cheque
shibbaak window
shibbaak ittazaakir ticket office
shimaal left (side)
shiwayya a little/some
shukran thanks!
shurb drinking
shurba soup
shurTa police

ta'reeban almost, about
taalit third
taamin eighth
taani second (2nd)
taasiε ninth
taεbaan not well/tired
taghyeer changing
taksi taxi
talaata, talat three
talateen thirty
talaTTaashar thirteen
taman, tamanya eight
tarabeiza table
tazkara (tazaakir) ticket
teen figs
tibda' start (f.)
ti'oom departs/takes off
tiHibb would you like . . . ?
tilifizyoun television
tilifoun telephone
tilt one third

tintihi ends (f.)
timsaal figure, statue
tisaεTaashar nineteen
tisεa, tissaε nine
tisεeen ninety
tiSbaH εala kheir goodnight!

Taabiε postage stamp
Tabεan of course
Tabeeb doctor
Talab (Talabaat) order (n.)
Tayyaara aeroplane
Tayyib yes! O.K.

'uddaam in front of
'urayyib/a near
'urS (a'raaS) pill
'usbooε week
'uTn Tibbi cotton wool

waaHid one (m.)
waHda one (f.)
walad boy
walla or
wi and
wibaεdein and then
wuSool arrival

ya a word used when addressing
    somebody
ya kamaal Kamaal!
yafandim sir!/madam!
yamadaam madam!
yi'oom departs (m.)
yibda' starts (m.)
yimeen right (side)
yintihi ends (m.)
youm day

zimeel/a colleague (m./f.)
ziyaara visit (n.)
zoug/a spouse (m./f.)

VOCABULARY

ARAB COUNTRIES

Country		Nationality	Capital	Currency
1	Algeria	'ljazaa'ir	jazaa'iri/ya*	'ljazaa'ir	'id-deenaar
2	Bahrain	'ilbaHrein	baHreini/ya	'ilmanaama	'id-deenaar
3	Egypt	maSr	maSri/ya	'ilqaahira	'il-gineih
4	Iraq	'ileiraaq	eiraaqi/ya	baghdaad	'id-deenaar
5	Jordan	'il'urdunn	'urduni/ya	eammaan	'id-deenaar
6	Kuwait	'ilkuweit	kuweiti/ya	'ilkuweit	'id-deenaar
7	Lebanon	libnaan	libnaani/ya	bayroot	'il-lira
8	Libya	leebya	leebi/ya	Tarablus	'id-deenaar
9	Mauritania	muritanya	muritaani/ya	nuwaakshuT	'il-'ookiya
10	Morocco	'ilmaghrib	maghribi/ya	'irribaaT	'id-dirham
11	Oman	eumaan	eumaani/ya	masqaT	'r-riyaal
12	Qatar	gaTar	gaTari/ya	'iddouHa	'r-riyaal
13	Saudi Arabia	'issaeoodiya	saeoodi/ya	'irriyaaD	'r-riyaal
14	Somalia	'sSumaal	Sumaali/ya	mugadeeshyu	'ish-shilin
15	Sudan	'issudaan	sudaani/ya	'ilkharToom	'il-geneih
16	Syria	surya	soori/ya	dimishq	'il-lira
17	Tunisia	toonis	tunsi/unisiya	toonis	'id-deenaar
18	United Arab Emirates	'il'imaaraat ilearabiya ilmuttaHida	min + name of emirate	'abu zaby	'id-dirham
19	Yemen	'ilyaman	yamani/ya	Saneaa'	'r-riyaal

* **i/ya**. **i** is the ending for the masculine adjective (nationality) and **iya** is the ending for the feminine. e.g. **jazaa'iri** (m.) and **jazaa'iriya** (f.) **maSri** (m.) **maSriya** (f.)

91

There are different types of written Arabic. The type introduced in this section is the most commonly used for printing books, newspapers and magazines, and for writing signposts.

Only the basic features of written Arabic are given here, since this book uses a colloquial variety of Arabic and is meant to teach spoken Arabic. Some of the examples given in this section are inevitably taken from literary (written) Arabic.

Arabic is written from left to right. It has its own alphabet of 29 letters. Whether written in long hand, typed or printed, the letters are joined up to make words. There are no capital letters in Arabic, but there are different forms of each letter according to its position in the word: initial, middle or final.

The Arabic alphabet

A list of the letters of the Arabic alphabet is given below showing the three forms of each letter, the English transliteration, and the English equivalent where there is one.

Equivalent	Transliteration	Final	Middle	Initial	Arabic
Initial					
a, e, i, o, u	ı				ء
a	aa	ـا	ـ	ا	ا
b	b	ـب	ـبـ	بـ	ب
t	t	ـت	ـتـ	تـ	ت
'th' in 'thin'	(th)	ـث	ـثـ	ثـ	ث
g/j	g/(j)	ـج	ـجـ	جـ	ج
. . .	H	ـح	ـحـ	حـ	ح
. . .	kh	ـخ	ـخـ	خـ	خ
d	d	ـد	ـ	د	د
'th' in 'the'	(dh)	ـذ	ـ	ذ	ذ

ARABIC WRITING

Equivalent	Transliteration	Position			Arabic
		Final	Middle	Initial	
r	r	ـر	ر	ر	ر
z	z	ـز	ز	ز	ز
c/s	s	ـس	ـسـ	سـ	س
sh	sh	ـش	ـشـ	شـ	ش
s	S	ـص	ـصـ	صـ	ص
d*	D	ـض	ـضـ	ضـ	ض
t*	T	ـط	ـطـ	طـ	ط
. . .	Z	ـظ	ـظـ	ظـ	ظ
. . .	ε	ـع	ـعـ	عـ	ع
. . .	gh	ـغ	ـغـ	غـ	غ
f	f	ـف	ـفـ	فـ	ف
. . .	(q)	ـق	ـقـ	قـ	ق
c/k	k	ـك	ـكـ	كـ	ك
l	l	ـل	ـلـ	لـ	ل
m	m	ـم/م	ـمـ	مـ	م
n	n	ـن	ـنـ	نـ	ن
h	h	ـه/ه	ﻬ	هـ	ه
w	w	ـو	و	و	و
i/y	y	ـي	ـيـ	يـ	ي

An asterisk after an English letter on the list means it is equivalent when it is in some positions only.

A letter between brackets means the sound it represents is mainly used in formal speech and only rarely in colloquial Arabic.

All the letters of the Arabic alphabet represent consonants except the second letter ا which is a long vowel. The letters ي and و are also long vowels as well as consonants. The three long vowels are therefore represented by the letters ا, و, and ي.

The first letter ء is either carried on one of the long vowel symbols ي . و ا or stands alone on the line.

Examples
guz' جزء   fu'aad فؤاد   ra'ees رئيس   'ahlan أَهْلًا

ARABIC WRITING

Vowels are either short or long. Short vowels are represented by three vowel marks which are written above or below the consonant concerned.

Examples

su	سُ	bi	بِ	ka	كَ
zu	زُ	fi	فِ	ta	تَ
ku	كُ	ti	تِ	ba	بَ

Long vowels are represented by the same vowel marks followed by one of the three consonants ا , ي or و .

Examples

dukhool	دُخُول	teen	تين	baab	بَابْ
khuroog	خُرُوج	sheek	شيك	haat	هَاتْ

If a consonant is not followed by a vowel, it has the sign ْ above it.

Examples

mishmish	مِشْمِشْ	bansyoun	بَنْسِيُونْ	bint	بْنْتْ

Sometimes the short **a** and the long **aa** are represented by the letter ى instead of the letter ا , at the end of some words.

Examples

mustashfaa	مُسْتَشْفَى	mabna	مَبْنَى	ɛala	عَلَى

If a consonant is doubled, one letter only is written with the mark above it. This mark is called *shadda*.

Examples

dabboor	دَبُّور	Hawwid	حَوِّد	maHaTTa	مَحَطَّة

The doubling of consonants also happens when **il** (meaning *the*), is used with words which start with one of the following consonants: t ت th ث d د dh ذ r ر z ز s س sh ش S ص D ض T ط Z ظ l ل n ن .

Examples

issudaan	السُّودَان	inneel	النِّيل	issaaɛa	السَّاعَة

The (h/ﻪ) sound used at the end of some words to indicate they are feminine nouns or adjectives, is always written in its final form (ة , ـة), with two dots above it. In colloquial Arabic this sound is pronounced like the short vowel (a).

Examples

sifaara	سفَارَة	waHda	وَاحْدَة	maHaTTa	مَحَطَّة

ARABIC WRITING

Vowel marks are not usually used in newspapers, magazines or books. Only school books for native or foreign learners of Arabic use vowel marks. By the time learners pass the beginners stage they do not need these marks except in very rare cases.

Some useful words

The following are some of the words you will see on boards and signposts, in the airports, streets and shops. They are written in the normal joined form, and the letters they are made up of are given, as well as the English transliteration.

Examples

maTaar	Airport	م ط ا ر	مَطَار
ilquaahira	Cairo	ا ل ق ا هـ ر ة	الْقَاهِرَة
iskindiriyya	Alexandria	ا ل إس ك ـن د ر يّ ة	ألاسْكَنْدَريَّة
aSwaan	Aswan	أ س و ا ن	أسْوَان
luksur	Luxor	ا ل أ ق ص ر	الأقْصُر
wuSool	Arrival	و ص و ل	وُصُول
mughadra	Departure	م غ ا د ر ة	مُغَادَرَة
khuroog	Exit, out	خ ر و ج	خُرُوج
dukhool	Entry, way in	د خ و ل	دُخُول
algawazaat	Passport (control)	ا ل ج و ا ز ا ت	الْجَوَازَات
algumruk	Customs	ا ل ج م ر ك	الْجُمْرُك
bank	Bank	ب ن ك	بنك
'issooq ilHurra	Duty Free Shops	ا ل س و ق ا ل ح ر ة	السُوق الْحُرَّة
gineih	Pound	ج ن ي ه	جنيه
'irsh	Piastre	ق ر ش	قِرْش
dinaar	Dinar	د ي ن ا ر	دِينَار
dirham	Dirham	د ر هـ م	دِرْهَم
riyaal	Riyal	ر يَ ا ل	رِيَال
maHaTTa	Station	مـ ح ط ة	مَحَطَّة
sikka Hadeed	Railway	س ك ة ح د ي د	سكَّة حَديد
maw'af	Stop	م و ق ف	مَوْقَف
taksi	Taxi	ت ا ك س ي / أ ج ر ة	تاكسي / أُجْرَة
'utubees	Bus	أ ت و ب ي س	أتوبيس
tilifoun	Telephone	ت ل ي ف و ن	تليفون
huteil	Hotel	هـ و ت ي ل	هُوتيل
bansyoun	Boarding House	ب ن س ي و ن	بَنْسِيُون

beit shabaab	Youth Hostel	ب ي ت ش ب ا ب	بيتْ شَبَاب
'ism ishshurTa	Police Station	ق س م ال ش رط ة	قِسْم الشُّرْطَة
'issifaara . . .	The . . . Embassy	ال سّ ف ا رة	السِّفَارة...
ilbireeTaaniyya	British	ا ل ب ري ط ا ن يّ ة	البريطانيّة
maTɛam	Restaurant	م ط ع م	مَطْعَم
maktaba	Library/Stationers	م ك ت ب ة	مَكْتَبَة
mustashfa	Hospital	م س ت ش ف ى	مُسْتَشْفَى
Saydaliyya	Pharmacy	ص ي د ل ي ة	صَيْدَلِيَّة
maktab bareed	Post Office	م ك ت ب ب ر ي د	مَكْتَب بَريد
'ahwa	Café	ق ه ـ و ة	قَهْوَة
shaariɛ	Street	ش ا ر ع	شارع
midaan	Square/Place	م ي د ا ن	مِيْدان
keelu	Kilo	ك ـ ي ل و	كيلو